Dancing for Fun

Dancing for Fun

Group Dancing for All Ages

Book Two

Piano Compositions by
Mark L. Greathouse

Choreography Transcriptions by
Helena Greathouse

iUniverse

DANCING FOR FUN
GROUP DANCING FOR ALL AGES

iUniverse books may be ordered through booksellers or by contacting:

iUniverse
1663 Liberty Drive
Bloomington, IN 47403
www.iuniverse.com
1-800-Authors (1-800-288-4677)

ISBN: 978-1-4917-5611-9 (sc)
ISBN: 978-1-4917-5612-6 (e)

Library of Congress Control Number: 2015900524

Print information available on the last page.

iUniverse rev. date: 3/17/2015

To all dancers
who wish to learn new dance skills while having fun

Contents

Preface

Dancing is part of being human. Our earliest ancestors moved their bodies to the accompaniment of rhythms and chants. This urge to move together with sounds or music is part of our human nature.

This book, second in the series, presents dances in which you can express your deepest feelings together with music. If you want to dance in a group of any size, at any age, you can easily do it using this book. To benefit the most, however, some intermediate level dancing is recommended.

The online YouTube videos show you how to perform the moves. Go to our website www.greathouseofmusic.com and click the tab "Dancing for Fun, Book 2." At the back of the book, you will find the links to YouTube, where you can see each dance performed. The written choreography for each dance is presented in this book **for reference** to match the dance exactly with the music. As with book one, these dances are meant to be done in a group, which invites having a lot of fun with other dancers. The dances are not in any particular order, so just pick a dance and start learning it. Check the glossary at the back of the book to learn the meaning of the underlined words that you'll find throughout.

When we prepared this book, we wanted to make sure that you could learn the dance as easily as possible and have fun at the same time. Now give it a try!

We especially wish to thank the following: Marilyn Olson, who ultimately inspired the creation of the music and who contributed many hours to the editing of the music—without her help there would be no music; Elena Kameníková, for the creation and performance of the choreography; Gail Watson, for her skills in designing the book; Elizabeth Berg, for her artistic contribution for the front cover; and Ron Stark, for his technical knowledge and computer skills and for his generosity in giving his time.

Introduction

Over the years Mark has had an ongoing interest in composing melodies, especially on the piano. Nevertheless, he performs on the accordion as a soloist and accompanies Helena's singing and dancing. They perform at many locations in Oregon as well as in Helena's native country, the Czech Republic, and in Slovakia and Germany. Over the years, whenever a new melody would come to Mark, he would record it on a cassette tape. This activity began in the 1980s and continues to the present. Later in 2009 Mark began to transcribe these melodies into notation form, and under the guidance of composer Marilyn Olson of Newberg, Oregon, it became apparent that many of these melodies could be easily used for dance. This combination of melody and dance has led to the writing of this second book in the series *Dancing for Fun*.

Helena brings special abilities to our duo, the Greathouse of Music. In the case of this book, she thoroughly understands the choreography of these dances. Elena Kameníková of Prague created all of the choreography, and then Helena, observing each dance, transcribed it all into English from their conversations in their mutual native language, Czech.

Helena competed in rhythmic gymnastics for twelve years, until the end of her university years. She coached this sport, and then for twenty-nine years she judged rhythmic gymnastics, representing the United States as an international judge (two Olympics, the Goodwill Games, the Pan American Games). She therefore knows well the dance terminology and techniques represented in this book.

There are no restrictions on the performance of these dances. Feel free to show them to audiences wherever, whenever! If you put them on YouTube, the world can see them— including us. We would be proud!

How to Use This Book

This book is intended for dancers in a group who are intermediate in their skill level. The first two dances are relatively easy, but to get the maximum benefit of this book, dancers should have had some dance practice. There is no progressive order of difficulty to the dances in the book. Just take a look at the table below and the dances online. Choose one that you particularly like.

It would be good to have a dance leader or instructor become familiar with the dance before the group practice begins. This person could watch the online dancer beforehand and then give personalized guidance to the other dancers as they learn the dance.

Below are a few points which will help you maximize the use of this book.

♫ These are all group dances with a minimum of at least two dancers but preferably more in order to create more of a group activity. More dancers will show the dances to be more beautiful and even more fun to learn.

♫ For the most part, the level of dance is intermediate. Some dance experience is advisable.

♫ The dances are all relatively short, all being less than four minutes.

♫ Be sure to note the starting formation and starting position at the beginning of each dance.

♫ In some dances the dancers are divided into two groups: odd and even. In these instances there is different choreography for each group (mirror image). Only the dance Trekking has video of both versions. In other dances, if odd and even groups are mentioned, the video shows the choreography for only one group, but the choreography is written for both.

♫ Read the choreography before starting each dance because the video only shows one dancer.

♫ Adjust formations based on the actual number of dancers you have.

♪ The table below will give you some information for each dance in the book. This can be helpful when it comes to planning and organizing each dance.

♪ Check out our website (www.greathouseofmusic.com) to hear other musical forms (vocal, solo piano, accordion) of some of the music in this book.

Name of Dance	Level of Difficulty	Special Notes
Who Cares?	Easy	Choreography is written for eight dancers.
Trekking	Easy	There are two videos: one for even-numbered dancers and one for odd-numbered dancers.
Reflections	Easy-intermediate	Dance calls for three rows of dancers.
Innocence Waltz	Intermediate	Dance calls for three rows of dancers.
Portraits	Advanced-intermediate	There are odd- and even-numbered dancers. Choreography is written for eight dancers.
Clown Dance	Advanced-intermediate	There are odd- and even-numbered dancers. Choreography is written for six dancers.
Remembrance	Advanced-intermediate	Three rows of dancers
Muffin Rag	Intermediate	Three rows of dancers
Snowfall	Advanced-intermediate	There are odd- and even-numbered dancers.
Medieval Waltz, part 1	Advanced-intermediate	One dancer is designated as soloist. Use a scarf.
Medieval Waltz, part 2	Advanced-intermediate	Soloist and odd- and even-numbered dancers
Medieval Waltz, part 3	Intermediate	Soloist
Medieval Waltz, part 4	Intermediate	Soloist
Medieval Waltz, part 5	Advanced-intermediate	Soloist. Use a scarf.

Choreography

Elena Kameníková

Elena Kameníková, dance teacher at
Taussigova Performance Arts School, Prague, Czech Republic.

Since early childhood, I have been active in dance and rhythmic gymnastics. As a rhythmic gymnast, I was a member of a competitive group that twice received the title of Junior Champion of the Czech Republic.

In 1991 I entered Jaroslav Jezek Dance Conservatory in Prague. Upon graduation I started to dance in the ballet of the State Opera in Prague, first in the ensemble and later as a soloist. Later I transferred as a soloist to the ballet company of F.X. Salda in Liberec, Czech Republic.

Between 2000 and 2003 I studied at the School of Philosophy at Charles University in Prague, receiving a bachelor of arts degree.

Who Cares?

Daily life surely has its frustrations—

but being a caring friend to all and extending

love unconditionally brings us closer to

peace and happiness. Try it!

Who Cares?

Dancing for Fun
Book 2

Jauntily

Mark L. Greathouse

Dance 1: Who Cares? Choreography

Key Signature: 4/4

Introduction: none

Starting formation: Dancers *face audience in staggered lines* so that all dancers can be seen by the audience. Ideally there should be an even number of dancers.

Starting position: Stand on left, right leg crossed in front of left, right ankle touching left leg, toes flat on floor, right heel up, arms behind back, one hand in palm of other and resting against lower back, head down.

Measures 1–2: Starting on count 2 of measure 1, turn 360 degrees to left on toes, feet together. Arms remain behind back.

Measure 3: Turning forty-five degrees to right to *face right diagonal*, chassé step right with slight side bend of body to right.

Measure 4: Turning ninety degrees to left to *face left diagonal*, repeat measure 3 but to opposite side.

Measure 5:

> Counts 1–2: Turning forty-five degrees to right to *face audience*, shift weight to left leg forward; slight demi-plié on left; right leg executes front cou-de-pied.

> Counts 3–4: Step back right, shifting weight to right; right knee is straight; left leg front on pique.

Measure 6:

> Counts 1–2: Slight demi-plié on right. Left leg executes front cou-de-pied.

> Counts 3–4: Same as counts 3–4 in measure 5 but to opposite side.

Note: During measures 5-6, lift arms gradually through sides to overhead into <u>third position of arms</u>; head remains looking forward.

Measures 7-8: Leg movement is same as in measures 1-2. This means in count 1 of measure 7 legs reach starting position of the dance and arms remain in <u>third position of arms</u>. Then gradually open arms to sides and lower them to position of arms at start of dance. At the end of measure 8, legs are in <u>first (I) position</u>.

Measures 9-14: Repeat movement of measures 3-8.

Measure 15:

Count 1: Slight <u>demi-plié</u> on left; right <u>leg</u> front <u>on pique</u>.

Count 2-4: Stretched right leg moves to side and back, describing 270-degree arc to right with toes on floor, while body turns ninety degrees to right to finish with **left shoulder to audience**. Arms gradually rise sideways to side low.

Measure 16: Through <u>fourth (IV) position</u> shift weight back to right leg, and through <u>demi-plié</u> straighten both legs so that at end of measure, dancer stands on right with left <u>leg</u> front <u>on pique</u>. Left arm continues to rise to the side horizontal. Right arm rises to forward horizontal. This is achieved by a slight inward circling of the arms. During movement, the head turns to left; perform a slight <u>dorsal backbend</u>.

Measure 17: Stepping forward on left, slide right through <u>first (I) position</u> and <u>cat leap</u> right. In the air, legs move as follows: right leg stretched forward low, left leg bent. Arms repeat slight inward circles as in measure 16.

Measure 18: Straighten both legs to stand on right; left <u>leg</u> front <u>on pique</u> and repeat movement of measure 17.

Measures 19-20: Straighten both legs to stand on right; left <u>leg</u> front <u>on pique</u> and shift weight forward to <u>lunge</u> on left. Then turn 270 degrees to right on left by straightening the left knee and sliding stretched right leg to the left. Finish **facing audience** in <u>fifth (V) position</u> <u>relevé</u>, right leg front. Arms gradually rise through sides to overhead to <u>third position of arms</u>.

Measure 21: Side bend to left. Slide right leg to side on floor, and through <u>second (II) position</u> demi-plié, shift weight to right, finishing in side bend to left (<u>side body wave</u> right). From overhead describing semicircle in frontal plane, swing arms to left, down, and then to right. Head follows movement of arms.

Measure 22: Repeat side body wave from measure 21 to opposite side while swinging arms in frontal plane down and then to left. Head follows movement of arms.

Measure 23: Repeat movement of measure 22 to opposite side.

Measure 24: Shift weight to demi-plié on left, turning 180 degrees to left, stretched right leg sliding along floor to left leg. Finish in first (I) position with **back to audience**. Gradually lower arms during turn, and at end of this measure place them behind back as described in starting position.

Measure 25: Chassé step on left, moving forward and away from audience.

Measure 26: Turning ninety degrees to right, **right shoulder to audience**, chassé step on right, moving forward in direction parallel with audience.

Measure 27: Turning ninety degrees to right to **face audience**, chassé step on left, moving forward toward audience.

> Note: During measures 25, 26, and 27, arms remain behind back, as described in starting position.

Measure 28: Through slight demi-plié on left, right leg side on pique, step right side on relevé and execute 360-degree soutenu turn to right, finishing **facing audience** in fifth (V) position relevé, right leg front. During turn, raise arms through front into third position of arms overhead.

Measure 29: Repeat movement of measure 21 as written (side body wave right).

Measure 30: Repeat movement of measure 24 as written (turn 180 degrees to left), finishing with **back to audience**.

Measures 31–32: Execute four steps (right, left, right, left), describing half circle to right so that at the end of the fourth step, dancer is **facing audience**. Arms port de bras, finishing as in starting position.

Measure 33:

> Counts 1–2: Prepare cou-de-pied, right leg behind left, and through step right back, small hop on right, left stretched forward at forty-five degrees.

Counts 3-4: Step left back and repeat same hop on left.

Measure 34:

Counts 1-2: Step right back and repeat same hop on right.

Counts 3-4: Step left back and repeat same hop on left.

Note: During measures 33 and 34 arms remain in starting position.

Measures 35-36: Execute four steps (right, left, right, left), describing 270-degree arc to right, so that at the end of fourth step, dancer finishes with **right shoulder to audience**. Arms remain as in starting position.

Measure 37:

Counts 1-2: Step right front and hop on right, left leg in <u>parallel</u> front <u>cou-de-pied.</u>

Counts 3-4: Repeat movement of counts 1-2 to opposite side.

Measure 38: Repeat movement of measure 37.

Note: Traveling during measures 37-38 is done in a ninety-degree arc to the left so that dancers finish with their **backs to audience**.

Measures 39-40: Take four walking steps (right, left, right, left), describing half circle to the left so that the dancers finish in **single-file facing audience** at end of measure 40. It will be necessary for each dancer to take steps of varying lengths in order to achieve this formation. Legs finish in <u>first (I) position</u>. Arms remain as in starting position.

Note: Measures 41-44 assume there are four pairs of dancers.

Measure 41:

Movement of dancer one: Turning ninety degrees to left **with right shoulder to audience**, <u>lunge</u> left front, and by straightening left knee and rising to left <u>relevé</u>, turn 270 degrees on left to left, right stretched leg sliding along floor to left. At end of turn, lower heels so that dancer finishes in <u>first (I) position</u> **facing audience**. During <u>lunge</u>, left arm low front, right arm low side. During turn, <u>first position of arms</u>. During lowering heels from <u>relevé</u>, make small circles from elbows down toward body, arms parallel to each other. Continue arm circles up away from body with palms up. Finish with lowering arms to body.

Movement of dancer two: Same movements as dancer one but to opposite side, so that dancers move away from each other. Dancer two, who began by standing behind dancer one, must execute movement slightly to right diagonal, so that at end of measure, both dancers are in **same line** *facing audience*.

Note: Dancers three through eight are standing in place without movement.

Measure 42: Dancers three and four execute movement of dancers one and two of measure 41. All other dancers stand in place without movement.

Measure 43: Dancers five and six execute movement of dancers one and two of measure 41. All other dancers stand in place without movement.

Measure 44: Dancers seven and eight execute movement of dancers one and two of measure 41. All other dancers stand in place without movement.

Note: After measure 44 all dancers are in **two single-files** *facing audience*.

Measure 45: All dancers execute side body wave away from center.

Measure 46: All dancers execute side body wave toward center.

Measure 47: Repeat movement of measure 45.

Measure 48:

Odd-numbered dancers repeat movement of dancer one from measure 41 (turn) but to opposite side.

Even-numbered dancers repeat movement of dancer one from measure 41 as written.

Note: At end of this measure, dancers are still in **two single-files** *facing audience*.

Musical interlude

Measure 49: First pair executes <u>chassé step</u> on inside leg followed by step forward with inside leg. Then close outside leg to inside leg. Entire movement is performed ***diagonally forward*** away from each other. Arms are in starting position (behind back). All other pairs remain standing in two single-files.

Measure 50: Second pair does same as first pair in previous measure. All other dancers remain in place.

Measure 51: Third pair does same as second pair in previous measure. All other dancers remain in place.

> Note: In measures 49–51 first pair executes the longest steps. Each succeeding pair takes shorter steps, so that at the end of measure 51 the group is in **V formation**, open toward the audience.

Measure 52:

> First pair: stretch right <u>leg</u> side <u>on pique</u>; then step on right <u>relevé,</u> and closing stretched left to right, turn 360 degrees to right, finishing in <u>first (I) position relevé</u> ***facing audience***. Arms remain in starting position behind back.

> Second pair: Same as first pair but to opposite side.

> Third pair: Same as first pair.

> Fourth pair: Same as second pair.

> Note: In measure 52 V formation is dissolved. All dancers finish in four parallel **staggered rows *facing audience***. Therefore, some dancers must take longer steps than others to achieve this formation.

Measure 53: Repeat measure 33 (dancers execute hops backward, starting with right).

Measure 54: Dancers change direction of movement, now executing hops forward toward audience, starting with right. In each hop, free leg in <u>cou-de-pied</u> behind hopping leg.

Measure 55:

> Counts 1–2: Step right side and hop on right, left leg stretched to side low.

Counts 3-4: Crossing left leg behind right, hop on left, right leg in front in low attitude.

Note: During measures 53-55 arms remain in starting position behind back.

Measure 56: Step right side on relevé, 360-degree soutenu turn to right. Finish **facing audience** in fifth (V) position relevé, right leg front. During turn, gradually raise arms through front to third position of arms.

Measures 57-60: Repeat measures 53-56 to opposite side.

Exception: The turn in measure 60 is only 180 degrees, finishing in first (I) position relevé with **back to audience**. Arms side low during measure 60.

Measures 61-64: Repeat movement from measures 25-28, traveling in a square.

Exception: During the soutenu turn in measure 64, keep arms down as in starting position and make turn forty-five degrees shorter, so that dancers finish **facing left diagonal**.

Measures 65-67: Take six walking steps in circle to right, beginning with right leg, finishing forty-five degrees short of full circle, with **right shoulder to audience**. Arms port de bras to front low and open to side low.

Measure 68: Cross right leg over left and turn 270 degrees to left on both feet in relevé, finishing in first (I) position relevé **facing audience**. Raise arms sideways up, finishing in third position of arms overhead. Look forward.

End of musical interlude

Measures 69-70: Lower heels from relevé to first (I) position. Lower arms sideways to starting position behind back.

Measures 71-115: Repeat movement of measures 3-47.

Measure 116: Right lunge to side and turn ninety degrees to right with **left shoulder to audience**. Then turn on flat foot 225 degrees (half circle plus forty-five degrees) to right to finish **facing left diagonal**. During turn, close left to right, left knee slightly bent forward. Finish standing on stretched right, left leg bent at knee, left on ball of foot, head down, arms crossed on chest, fingers touching shoulders.

Trekking

Moving deliberately forward at a

measured pace is often the way to overcome

obstacles and arrive at our life's purpose.

Trekking

Dancing For Fun
Book 2

Grandly

Mark L. Greathouse

Dance 2: Trekking Choreography

Key Signature: 4/4

Introduction: 1 note

> Note: Assume even number of dancers. If odd number, one dancer can be together with another in a couple.

Starting formation: Dancers in V formation, point of "V" closest to audience.

Starting position: Stand on left, right <u>leg</u> back <u>on pique</u>, arms side low. All dancers **face right back diagonal**.

> Note: On introductory note, dancers remain in place.

Measure 1: Without taking a step, turn 180 degrees to right on <u>supporting</u> left <u>leg</u> to **right front diagonal**. Then bend left <u>supporting leg</u> into <u>demi-plié</u>, right <u>leg</u> front <u>on pique</u>. Arms remain side low.

Measure 2: Step right front on <u>relevé</u>. Close left to right to <u>fifth (V) position</u> <u>relevé</u>, right leg front, arms move through front to <u>third position of arms</u>.

Measure 3: Turning forty-five degrees to left to **face audience**, <u>demi-plié</u> on left and <u>balance step</u> side right. Twist torso to right, keeping arms horizontal so that left arm is front and right arm is back. Look over left shoulder to audience.

Measure 4: Through <u>demi-plié</u> on right and left <u>leg</u> side <u>on pique</u>, step side left on <u>relevé</u> and <u>soutenu turn</u> 360 degrees to left, finish **facing audience** in <u>third (III) position</u> <u>relevé</u>, left leg front. Lower arms through <u>first position of arms</u> and then raise arms to front and to <u>third position of arms</u>. Finally, lower left heel to finish standing on left, turned out bent right leg on ball of foot touching left leg; lower arms to side horizontal.

Measure 5: Moving forward toward audience, step right, step left. Start with <u>arms in frontal plane</u> to left. Keeping left arm horizontal, right arm continues describing circle in <u>frontal plane</u> up and to right. Head first looks to left and then follows right arm when finishing circle above head.

Measure 6: <u>Demi-plié</u> on left and step forward on right <u>relevé</u>, closing left to right to <u>fifth (V)</u> <u>position</u> <u>relevé</u>, right leg front. Arms through front to <u>third position of arms</u>. Look forward.

Measure 7: Through <u>cou-de-pied</u> step left back into <u>demi-plié</u> on left, right <u>leg</u> front <u>on</u> <u>pique</u>, "bowing position," left arm front horizontal, right arm side, torso tilted forward and straight, head in line with torso.

> Note: Beginning with measure 8, dancers are divided into **odd numbered** **on left side of the V formation** (from dancers' point of view) and **even numbered on right side of the V formation**.

> Note: In measures 8–22 movement of odd-numbered dancers is different from movement of even-numbered dancers.

Measure 8:

> **Odd-numbered dancers** on left side: cross right leg over left and turn in <u>relevé</u> 270 degrees to left, finishing in <u>first (I) position</u> with **left shoulder to** **audience**, arms side low.

> **Even-numbered dancers** on right side: same as odd-numbered dancers except turn is only ninety degrees to left, finishing with **right shoulder to** **audience**.

> Note: At end of measure 8, there are two lines of dancers **in original V** **formation. Dancers face each other.**

Measures 9–10: Repeat movement of measures 5–6 (walking with arm movement in <u>frontal</u> <u>plane</u> and <u>relevé</u>), but each line is the **mirror image** of the other, **lines moving toward each** **other**.

> **Odd-numbered dancers** on left side: opposite legs move in same direction and fashion as in measures 5–6.

> **Even-numbered dancers** on right side: opposite arms move in same direction and fashion as in measures 5–6.

> Note: In measure 9 all dancers look toward audience during frontal circle with arm.

Measures 11–12: Repeat movements of measures 7–8 ("bowing position" and turn), but each line is the **mirror image** of the other, **lines moving away from each other**.

> Note: In "bowing position" of measure 11, all dancers look toward audience and are in demi-plié on leg away from audience, with arm away from audience in front and other arm to side.

> Note: The turn in measure 12 is 360 degrees for all dancers in the direction away from the audience, finishing with **both lines facing each other**.

Measures 13–14:

> **Odd-numbered dancers** on left side: repeat measures 3–4 (balance step and soutenu turn), but soutenu turn is only 270 degrees, finishing with **back to audience**.

> **Even-numbered dancers** on right side: same as odd-numbered dancers (mirror image) but to opposite side, finishing with **back to audience**.

> **Notes to measures 15–22**:

> Note 1: In measures 15–22 dancers form one **single-file *facing audience***, so that first dancer from left side is number one in line, first dancer from right side is number two, second dancer from left side is number three, second dancer from right side is number four, etc.

> Note 2: Dancers then move to opposite side from which they came.

> Note 3: Dancers then return to the same single-file described in Note 1.

> Note 4: Dancers then return to their original places.

Measures 15–16: With walking steps, dancers form one line as described in Note 1 above.

Odd-numbered dancers start walking with right leg and walk in an arc to the left, gradually turning 180 degrees so that they finish ***facing audience***.

Even-numbered dancers start walking with left and walk in an arc to the right, gradually turning 180 degrees so that they finish ***facing audience***.

Note: Measures 17–20: **Even-numbered dancers**: same as odd-numbered dancers but to opposite side, always facing audience.

Measures 17–18: **Odd-numbered dancers**: grapevine step to right, starting with crossing left behind right. While moving to right, cross left one more time in front of right, and then one more time cross left behind right, and finally cross left in front of right, putting weight on left, and stop (twisting hips accordingly). Arms side low.

Measures 19–20: **Odd-numbered dancers**: repeat measures 17–18 to opposite side, moving to left with the following change: finish in first (I) position *facing audience*.

Note: After measure 20, **all dancers are again in single-file *facing audience***.

Note: Measures 21–22: **Even-numbered dancers**: same as odd-numbered dancers but to opposite side.

Measures 21–22: **Odd-numbered dancers**: turn forty-five degrees to left to lunge on left, *facing left diagonal*. Execute chaines turning to left along left diagonal. After each 360-degree turn, start to step into lunge on left and continue chaines. This means dancers turn 360 degrees once and 315 degrees once, finishing in first (I) position *facing audience*. Arms close to body.

Note: After measure 22, **all dancers are in original V formation** as at the beginning of dance. Dancers must take steps of varying lengths to reach this formation.

Note: In measures 23–40 **all dancers do same movements, maintaining V formation**.

Measure 23: Demi-plié on left, right leg front on pique, and then step forward on right relevé and close left to right into fifth (V) position relevé, right leg front. Move arms through front to third position of arms.

Measure 24: Through cou-de-pied, step left back into demi-plié on left, right leg front on pique, "bowing position," left arm front horizontal, right arm side, torso tilted forward and straight, head in line with torso.

Measure 25: Cross right leg over left and turn in relevé 270 degrees to left, finishing in first (I) position with *left shoulder to audience*. Arms side low.

Measure 26: Turn ninety degrees to right to <u>lunge</u> on right with **back to audience** and <u>chaines</u> turning right (270 degrees altogether), traveling away from audience. Finish in <u>first (I) position</u> with **left shoulder to audience**, arms side low.

Measures 27–28: Four steps forward starting with right. During walking, turn 135 degrees to right. Finish on **right back diagonal**, standing on left, right <u>leg</u> back <u>on pique</u>. <u>Arms port de bras</u> through <u>first</u> and <u>second position</u>. Right arm continues close to body and subsequently front horizontal; left arm remains side horizontal.

Measures 29–40: Repeat measures 1–12 from beginning of dance, but the final <u>soutenu turn</u> is 270 degrees to finish **facing audience**.

Note: **Odd-numbered dancers** perform measures 41–44 as follows:

Measure 41: Repeat measure 3 (balance step side right) without initial turn (always facing audience) but change movement of arms to do arm swing from left to right in <u>frontal plane</u>; head follows arms.

Measure 42: Repeat measure 41 to opposite side, but look over right shoulder at the end of this measure.

Measure 43: Step side on right <u>relevé</u> and turn 315 degrees on right to right, left leg <u>cou-de-pied</u> in back of right, arms side low. Finish **facing left diagonal**.

Measure 44: Step left front, right <u>leg</u> back <u>on pique</u>. Keep arms side low.

Note: Measures 41–44: **Even-numbered dancers**: same movement as odd-numbered dancers but opposite side. Final position is **facing right diagonal**.

Reflections

Watch the sunlight shimmering on the

surface of a lake. Is your life a reflection

of your inner thoughts, beliefs, and values?

Reflections

Dancing For Fun
Book 2

Mark L. Greathouse

Dance 3: Reflections Choreography

Key Signature: 4/4

Introduction: none

Starting formation: Dancers begin in **staggered rows**.

Starting position: With **back to audience** stand on left, right leg crossed in front of left, right ankle touching left leg, toes pointed and touching floor, right heel up, arms side low.

Measure 1: With weight on both feet, turn on toes in <u>relevé</u>, 225 degrees (half circle plus forty-five degrees) to left (finishing **facing left diagonal**), simultaneously raising arms through sides to overhead into <u>third position of arms</u>.

Measure 2: Through <u>cou-de-pied</u> step left back, right <u>leg</u> front <u>on pique</u>. Lower right arm to side horizontal and left arm to front horizontal, palms up.

Measure 3:

    Counts 1–2: Step right forward.

    Counts 3–4: While turning ninety degrees to right to **face right diagonal**, cross left over right and step left forward.

    Note: During measure 3, arms are gradually lowered to sides of body.

Measure 4: While turning forty-five degrees to left to **face audience**, <u>cou-de-pied</u> right leg behind left. Step right side and side <u>lunge</u> on right. Right arm executes frontal circle down in front of body to overhead, stopping so that right arm, torso, and left leg form one line while <u>lunge</u> on right. Right arm with palm up; left arm side low, parallel with left leg.

Measure 5: By shifting weight to left, repeat movement of measure 3.

Measure 6: Step front right to <u>lunge</u> on right to **face right diagonal**. Through straightening right knee while rising on right <u>relevé</u>, left leg in low <u>arabesque</u>, turn 315 degrees (full circle minus 45 degrees) on right to right to **face audience**. At end of measure, close left to right to <u>relevé</u> in <u>first (I) position</u>. During turn, right arm diagonally front high, palm down, and left arm diagonally back low, parallel with left leg.

Measure 7:

> Counts 1–2: <u>Parallel demi-plié</u> with legs together, lower arms so that elbows touch torso, palms up front low. Through stepping right side, <u>relevé</u> in <u>second (II) position</u>. Through swiveling elbows outward, raise arms, leaving lower arms loose, palms down, fingers of one hand close to fingers of the other.

> Counts 3–4: By shifting weight to left and turning forty-five degrees to left to **face left diagonal**, <u>demi-plié</u> on left, close right leg left, right leg bent at knee, touching floor with ball of foot without weight. Through action of elbows, first up and then down, small circles of forearms first toward body and then up and away from body, palms up.

> Note: Movement of arms in measure 7 is graceful and continuous.

Measure 8: Step front right to <u>lunge</u> on right, lower arms close to body. By rising on right <u>relevé</u> while in <u>demi-plié</u> on right, turn 405 degrees (full circle plus forty-five degrees) to right to **face audience**. Execute turn in <u>demi-plié</u> on right, left leg in low <u>arabesque</u>, left toes touching floor. At end of turn, move left leg from back to left side. Hold hands together behind body at low back.

Measure 9: Turn ninety degrees to right with **left shoulder to audience**, and through small <u>develope</u>, step left front. Release hands and move both arms to side low. By closing right ankle to left calf, turn 180 degrees to left in <u>demi-plié</u> on left, finishing with **right shoulder to audience**. During turn bring elbows to touch body, forearms front high, palms up. At end of turn, head down.

Measure 10: Through raising right leg to parallel <u>passé</u> front, <u>develope</u> right leg back to horizontal, <u>demi-plié</u> on left (<u>support leg</u>). Move torso forward so that torso is in one line with right leg. Left arm front parallel with floor, palm down; right arm back parallel with floor, palm down.

> Note: Measures 11–12 assume there are **three rows of dancers**.

Measure 11:

Counts 1-2: **First row:** straighten torso to vertical, swing straight right leg forward to low front, brushing left <u>support leg</u> in process. Step on right <u>relevé</u> front, closing left leg to right into <u>fifth (V) position</u> <u>relevé</u>, right leg front. Lower arms close to body and then raise them to front horizontal. Put one palm into the other and bend elbows toward body in circular motion inward, downward, and then upward to arms high front. Head follows arm movement.

Second and third rows: straighten torso to vertical, maintain <u>lunge</u> on left, right leg stretched back, toes touching floor; *body weight remains on left leg.* Lower arms to side of body.

Counts 3-4: **First row:** hold final position of measure 11, counts 1-2.

Second row: same as movement of row 1 of measure 11, counts 1-2.

Third row: Continue holding <u>lunge</u> from measure 11, counts 1-2.

Measure 12:

Counts 1-2: **First and second rows:** continue holding final position of measure 11.

Third row: Same as movement of row 1 of measure 11, counts 1-2.

Counts 3-4: all dancers hold final position of measure 12, counts 1-2.

Note: In measures 11 and 12 dancers are with ***right shoulder to audience*** and perform movement in <u>canon.</u>

Note: From this point on movement is same for all dancers.

Measure 13: By lowering heels to floor and crossing left leg over right, turn 180 degrees to right in <u>relevé</u>, dancers with ***left shoulder to audience***. Bend elbows outward and then circle forearms forward, downward, and inward toward body; release hands and finish circle so that arms are horizontal front, palms up.

Measure 14: Two <u>chaines</u> to right (right, left, right, left) of various lengths, so that at end of measure **dancers form a circle** with *right shoulder toward center of circle*. <u>First position of arms</u>.

Measure 15: Open arms to sides. Step right side to side <u>lunge</u> on right. Right arm executes frontal circle down in front of body to overhead, stopping so that right arm, torso, and left leg form one line while <u>lunge</u> on right. Right arm with palm up, left arm side low, parallel with left leg.

Measure 16: Step left, cross right leg over left and turn to left, finishing in <u>first (I) position</u>, so that dancers have ***backs toward audience***. Through lowering arms, bend elbows outward and then circle forearms downward and inward toward body, finishing circle so that arms are horizontal front, palms up. By performing this, dancers dissolve circle and are again **in rows**.

Measure 17:

> Counts 1–2: Step right back, left <u>leg</u> front <u>on pique</u>. Left arm to side horizontal, head follows movement of left arm.

> Counts 3–4: Repeat same to other side, continuing to move back toward audience.

Measure 18: Bending right knee, slide right leg along floor toward left leg. With slight impulse of right toes from floor, turn 225 degrees to right on left (flat foot); finish turn ***facing right diagonal***. At end of turn, left <u>support leg</u> in <u>demi-plié</u>, through <u>cou-de-pied,</u> stretch right leg front <u>on pique</u>, toes touching floor. Through <u>first position of arms</u>, open right arm to side, raise left arm through front up, head follows left arm.

Measure 19: Take two steps (right, left) along right diagonal. Lower arms to body.

Measure 20: Step forward right to <u>lunge</u> on right. Repeat <u>arabesque</u> turn from measure 6, and finish ***facing audience***.

> Note: Only first row of dancers move during measures 21–22. Remaining dancers stand without movement. During measures 23–24, remaining dancers do movement of first-row dancers from measures 21–22.

Measure 21 **(first-row dancers):**

> Counts 1-2: Step right side to <u>relevé</u> in <u>second (II) position</u>. Arms in fast movement: elbows together in front of torso, cross forearms, continuing to move them to sides. Dancers *face audience*.

> Counts 3-4: Turn ninety degrees to left, *right shoulder to audience*. Shift weight to left and close right leg to left, bending right knee, touching floor with ball of right foot. Head down, arms low next to torso.

Measure 22 **(first-row dancers):** Turn 135 degrees right, finishing *facing right diagonal*, and step right on diagonal, turning on right half <u>relevé</u> 360 degrees to right, left leg in <u>cou-de-pied</u> slightly turned out. During turn, one arm follows the other in movement, keeping arms continuously in one straight line—first right arm up with left keeping close to body and then left arm up with right arm close to body (<u>airplane arms</u>).

Measure 23 **(first-row dancers):** Step left front into <u>demi-plié</u> and straighten knee, right <u>leg back on pique</u>. Continue arm movement from previous measure with right arm up; keep left arm close to body and finish circle of right arm so that both arms are down close to body at end of this measure.

Measure 24 **(first-row dancers):** Rise on <u>relevé</u> on left and turn 325 degrees (as an option turn 360 degrees) to right, gradually sliding stretched right leg to left leg so that the turn is finished in <u>fifth (V) position</u> <u>relevé</u>, right leg front, *facing audience (as an option finish facing right diagonal)*. Arms down close to body.

> Measures 23-24 **(all remaining dancers):** Repeat movement of measures 21-22 for first-row dancers, except turn (on half <u>relevé</u>) of measure 22 is shortened to 315 degrees to finish *facing audience (as an option turn 360 degrees and finish facing right diagonal).*

> Note: From this point on movement is the same for all dancers.

Measure 25:

> Counts 1-2: Step left front and execute small <u>stag leap</u>, taking off from left. During leap, right leg bent front, left leg stretched back forty-five degrees, left arm front horizontal, right arm side horizontal.

> Counts 3-4: Repeat movement of counts 1-2.

Measure 26: Step left front to <u>lunge</u> on left; rise on <u>relevé</u> on left and turn 360 degrees (as an option turn 315 degrees) to right, gradually sliding stretched right leg to left leg so that the turn is finished in <u>fifth (V) position</u> relevé, right leg front ***facing audience***. During turn, arms gradually rise to <u>third position of arms</u>.

Measure 27:

> Counts 1-2: Step side left, through side bend right with impulse to left; execute half circle down with left arm in <u>frontal plane</u> close to body so that at end of measure arms are in one line with side bend of torso to right. Close right leg to left, so that support left leg is stretched and right knee bent parallel forward, right leg touching floor with ball of foot.

> Counts 3-4: Repeat movement of counts 1-2 to opposite side, but arms remain at sides, making soft movements to accompany movement of torso.

> Note: Throughout measure 27 all movement is constantly flowing, following impulses of torso.

Measure 28: Small step to left side. Crossing right over left turn 405 degrees (full circle plus forty-five degrees) in <u>relevé</u> to left. Arms close to side. Finish ***facing left diagonal***.

Measures 29-34: Repeat movement of measures 3-8 (includes <u>arabesque</u> turns). Finish ***facing audience***.

Measure 35: Repeat movement of measure 27 (side bends).

Measure 36: Cross right over left and turn 360 degrees to left in <u>relevé</u>, arms close to body.

Measure 37: Step side right on <u>relevé</u> in <u>second (II) position</u>; arms circle in <u>frontal plane</u> in front of body down, cross in front of body, and open to sides.

Measure 38: Step right front toward audience. Turn 360 degrees to right on right, left leg in <u>parallel</u> <u>cou-de-pied</u>, finishing in <u>first (I) position</u> ***facing audience***. With arms low side, execute slight swing of arms to right, finishing with arms next to hips at sides, palms turned back, elbows slightly bent to sides.

Measures 39-40: Repeat movement of measures 37-38.

> Note: For measures 41-42 assume there are **three rows of dancers**.

Measure 41:

Counts 1–2: **First row:** through <u>demi-plié</u> on right and slight bend of left knee, left leg touching floor with ball of foot, turn ninety degrees to left with ***right shoulder toward audience***. Step left forward; slide right leg to left leg; finish standing on stretched left leg, right leg <u>parallel</u> bent forward, ball of foot touching floor. Right arm circles up on side in <u>frontal plane</u> before body turns and down through front in <u>sagittal plane</u> after body turns.

Second and third rows: dancers remain standing in place.

Counts 3–4: **Second row:** repeat movement of first row of dancers in counts 1–2.

First and third rows of dancers remain standing in place.

Measure 42:

Counts 1–2: **Third row:** repeat movement of first row of dancers in measure 41, counts 1–2.

First and second rows of dancers remain standing in place.

Note: From this point on movement is same for all dancers.

Counts 3–4: Turn forty-five degrees to right to ***face left diagonal***, and step right front into right <u>launch</u>. Swing right arm from right to left in <u>horizontal plane</u> in front of body to prepare for next turn.

Measure 43: Turn 405 degrees (full circle plus forty-five degrees) on right to right, left leg in low <u>arabesque</u> behind body. Finish ***facing the audience*** in <u>first (I) position</u>. During turn, right arm up, left arm behind body.

Measure 44:

Counts 1–2: Step right back, left leg stretched low front. Left <u>arm wave</u> to side and then down close to body; head follows movement of left arm.

Counts 3–4: Repeat counts 1–2 to opposite side.

Measure 45: Step right front on relevé and close left to right to fifth (V) position relevé, right leg front, arms through front to third position of arms.

Measure 46: Step left back, right leg front on pique. Open arms through sides to close to body.

Measure 47: Step right front, turning forty-five degrees to right to **face right diagonal**. Then step left front on right diagonal. Right arm describes arc from right to left in horizontal plane in front of body, finishing with right forearm horizontal in front, close to body, left arm side.

Measure 48:

> Counts 1-2: Step right side to side lunge on right, **facing audience**. Right arm executes circle in frontal plane, starting down and finishing side. Head follows right arm.

> Counts 3-4: Shift weight to left, turning forty-five degrees to left to **face left diagonal**; close arms to body. Step front right on left diagonal, crossing arms in front, close to body.

Measure 49: Step left on left diagonal, right leg back on pique. Open arms to sides, dorsal backbend, head up.

Measure 50: Demi-plié on left, slide right leg to left, bending right knee and touching floor behind left leg with ball of right foot. Turn palms up and then lower arms close to body. Dorsal front bend, head down.

Measure 51: Straighten both knees, and standing on left, arabesque with raised right leg back. Straighten torso, head up, gradually arms to sides.

Measure 52: Collapse to final position of measure 50, turning palms up before lowering arms.

Measures 53-54: Repeat movement of measures 51-52.

Measures 55-60: Repeat movement of measures 3-8 (steps with arm circles, arabesque turn, turn in demi-plié). Finish **facing audience**.

Measure 61:

> Counts 1-2: Step left side and slide bent right leg to left leg; dorsal side bend right, left side arm wave to side high, head follows left arm.

Counts 3-4: Repeat movement of counts 1-2 to opposite side.

Measure 62: Shift weight to left leg and cross right over left, turning 450 degrees (one and a quarter circles) to left, finishing in first (I) position with **right shoulder to audience**. During turn, arms close to body.

Note: During measures 63-64 assume there are **three rows of dancers**.

Measure 63: **First row:** turning ninety degrees to right to **face audience**, execute chaines toward audience, first position of arms. Finish standing on left, right leg back on pique **facing right diagonal**.

Second and third rows of dancers remain standing in place.

Measure 64: First row of dancers remain standing in place.

Second and third rows: Repeat movement of first row of dancers from measure 63.

Note: From this point on movement is same for all dancers.

Measure 65:

Counts 1-2: Step right back along right diagonal, right arm front low, left arm side low.

Counts 3-4: Turning forty-five degrees to left to **face audience**, step left back away from audience, left arm front low, right arm side low.

Measure 66: Cross right over left and turn 360 to left, arms close to body. Finish in first (I) position **facing audience**.

Measure 67: Turning forty-five degrees to left to **face left diagonal**, step right on left diagonal. Turning ninety degrees to right to **face right diagonal**, step left on right diagonal.

Measure 68:

Counts 1-2: Step right to lunge on right. Straightening right knee while rising on right relevé, turn 180 degrees to right on right, left in low arabesque. Right arm front high, left arm back low. Finish facing **back right diagonal**.

Counts 3-4: Step left front, right leg back on pique, head down, arms back low.

innocence Waltz

Innocence provides a certain sense of
safety and courage. Is innocence ever lost
completely? Can we regain it through goodness?

Innocence Waltz

Dancing For Fun
Book 2

Flowing

Mark L. Greathouse

Dance 4: Innocence Waltz Choreography

Key Signature: 3/4

Introduction: one initial tone plus first 4 measures

Starting formation: Dancers *facing center of large circle*.

Starting position: Stand on right, left leg back on pique, arms side low.

Measure 1: Hold in starting position.

Measure 2: Cross left over right; turn 270 degrees to right in relevé, finishing in first (I) position, *right shoulder toward center of circle*. Arms remain side low.

Measure 3: Swing arms to left low in frontal plane and balance step right toward center of circle while swinging arms to right in frontal plane to side. Dorsal side bend left; head follows movement of arms.

Measure 4: Step left side to demi-plié and turn 180 degrees to left on flat foot, finishing in first (I) position with *left shoulder toward center of circle*, arms close to body.

Measure 5: Chaines to right, dissolving circle. At end of steps, all dancers are with *right shoulder to audience and the formation is as close as possible to staggered rows (assuming three rows)*.

Measure 6: Step left front on relevé. Close right leg to left in first (I) position relevé. Raise arms forward horizontal, elbows leading.

Measure 7: Through demi-plié on left, and shifting weight while stepping back to right demi-plié, close left to right to relevé in first (I) position. Keeping upper arms horizontal, circle forearms toward body and continue circle in sagittal plane outward from body, finishing with arms front horizontal, palms up. Then lower arms toward body, elbows leading. While stepping, turn head to right toward audience.

Measure 8: Repeat movement of measure 6 (first (I) position relevé).

Measure 9: Turn ninety degrees to right and <u>chaines</u> to right toward audience. Finish *facing audience*. Arms close to body, elbows slightly outward, fingers touching thighs.

> Note: By doing <u>chaines</u> in measure 5 and measure 9, dancers finish staggered in rows parallel with audience. This means that different dancers must take steps of varying lengths to achieve this formation.

Measures 10–11: Repeat movement of measures 6–7 (<u>first (I) position</u> <u>relevé</u> with arm movements but now *facing audience*). Since dancers are now facing audience, it is not necessary for them to turn head.

Measure 12: First turn ninety degrees to right. Then execute <u>soutenu turn</u> 270 degrees to right to finish *facing audience*. Arms side low.

Measure 13:

> Count 1: Execute very small leap sideways to right, taking off from left (right leg stretched in air; after landing on right, left stretched leg describes horizontal semi-circle low in front of body); during leap, frontal arc of left arm to side and up; head follows left arm.

> Count 2: Turning 180 degrees to right with *back to audience*, step left to side on <u>relevé</u>.

> Count 3: Turning ninety degrees to right with *right shoulder to audience*, close right leg to left into <u>first (I) position</u> <u>relevé</u>. Move <u>arms</u> to <u>first position</u>.

Measure 14:

> Count 1: Execute very small leap back, taking off from right (left leg stretched in air; after landing on left, bend right leg <u>parallel</u> front). Turn palms up, right arm front horizontal, left arm side horizontal.

> Count 2: Stretch right leg low back and step on right <u>relevé</u>, turning ninety degrees to right to *face audience*. Both arms to left horizontal, palms up.

> Count 3: Cross left leg over right, and turning forty-five degrees to right, step on left <u>lunge</u>, *facing right diagonal*. Hold position of arms from count 2; turn palms down.

Measure 15: Turn forty-five degrees to left to **face audience** and balance step right. Dorsal side bend to left, arms in frontal plane to right; head follows arms.

Measure 16: Repeat movement of measure 15 (without initial turn) to opposite side, still facing audience.

Measures 17–18: Turning ninety degrees to right, **left shoulder to audience**, repeat movement of measures 13–14 (small leaps), moving away from audience.

Measure 19: With left shoulder still toward audience, balance step right. Dorsal side bend to left, arms in frontal plane to right; head follows arms.

Measure 20: Through demi-plié on right and left leg side on pique, step on left relevé and soutenu turn 270 degrees to left, finishing with **back to audience**, to stand on left, bent turned out right leg behind left, ball of foot touching floor, arms side low.

Measure 21: In canon:

> Count 1: **First row:** turn 180 degrees to right to **face audience** and finish in fifth (V) position relevé, right leg front.
>
> **Second and third rows:** Hold final position of measure 20.
>
> Count 2: **Second row:** repeat movement of first row, count 1.
>
> **First and third rows:** Hold position from count 1.
>
> Count 3: **Third row:** repeat movement of first row, count 1.
>
> **First and second rows:** Hold position from count 2.

Measures 22–23: Repeat movement of measures 15–16 (balance steps) without initial turn of measure 15.

Measure 24: Turning ninety degrees to right with **left shoulder to audience**, step on right relevé and soutenu turn 270 degrees to right to finish **facing audience** in fifth (V) position relevé, right leg front. Close arms to body and raise them through front to third position of arms.

Measure 25: Stepping right front, balance step forward facing audience. Arms through sides close to body.

Measure 26:

Count 1: Taking off from left, small leap back onto left, finishing in forward lunge on left, right leg through turned out develope, stretch leg back on pique. Raise arms to front horizontal, elbows leading, palms down.

Count 2: Step right side on relevé, left leg stretched low side. Hold arms in position.

Count 3: Crossing left over right and turning forty-five degrees to right, step on left demi-plié facing **right diagonal**, arms in frontal plane to left.

Measure 27:

Count 1: Taking off from left, small leap forward onto right **along right diagonal**, bending in air first right knee and then left knee. Swing right arm in frontal plane to right and up. When arm is up, turn elbow to left and continue circle of right arm in frontal plane down. Keep left arm side horizontal.

Counts 2-3: With torso facing audience, cross left over right, step on left into lunge on left, right leg on pique back to left side (movement and entire body in frontal plane). Both arms to left, right palm up.

Measure 28: Soutenu turn 360 degrees to right by closing right leg to left. Finish **facing audience** in fifth (V) position relevé, right leg front, arms close to body.

Measures 29-30: Repeat measure 25 and 26 (balance step and small leap with develope).

Changes for measure 30:

Count 2: Turning ninety degrees to right to finish with **left shoulder to audience**, step right side on relevé, left leg stretched low side. Arms in frontal plane to left.

Count 3: Crossing left over right, step on left demi-plié. Arms remain as in count 2.

Measure 31: Balance step right. Through down, move arms in frontal plane to right; head follows arm movement.

Measure 32: Stepping left side on <u>relevé</u>, cross right leg over left and turn 450 degrees (one and a quarter circles) to left in <u>relevé</u>. Finish in <u>first (I) position</u> **facing audience**, arms close to body.

Measure 33: <u>Balance step</u> left. Arms first to sides and then right arm moves in <u>horizontal plane</u> to front; left arm remains side horizontal. Gradually twist torso to left, looking forward toward audience over right shoulder.

Measure 34: Repeat leg, torso, and head movement of measure 33 to opposite side, still facing audience. Arms move to right in <u>horizontal plane</u> to finish with right arm side horizontal, left arm front horizontal.

Measures 35–36: Stepping left side on <u>relevé</u>, <u>soutenu turn</u> 360 degrees to left. First close arms to body and then through front, <u>third position of arms</u>.

Measure 37: <u>Balance step</u> right. Through side left and down, move both <u>arms in frontal plane</u> to right. Head follows arm movement.

Measure 38: Repeat movement of measure 37 to opposite side, still facing audience.

    Change: Do not take last two steps, so that dancers finish standing on left, right leg <u>parallel</u> bent forward on ball of foot close to left.

Measure 39: Through side <u>lunge</u> on right, <u>chaines with dorsal side bends</u> moving to right, parallel with audience.

Measure 40: Turning ninety degrees to right with **left shoulder to audience**, step left, right leg stretched back to touch floor with ball of foot. Twist torso to left so that head turns toward audience, <u>arms in frontal plane</u> to left.

Measure 41: <u>Balance step</u> right, still with left shoulder to audience, <u>arms in frontal plane</u> to right; head follows arm movement.

Measure 42: Step side left, turning ninety degrees to right with **back to audience**, so that dancers finish standing on left, right leg <u>parallel</u> bent forward on ball of foot close to left. First close arms to body and then move <u>arms in frontal plane</u> to left. Turn head to right to look over right shoulder.

Measure 43: Repeat movement of measure 39 (<u>chaines with dorsal side bends</u>). Finish **with right shoulder to audience**.

Measure 44: Turning forty-five degrees to right to **face left diagonal**, step left onto <u>demi-plié</u> and <u>arabesque scale</u>, tilting torso forward, arms back. In final position, <u>working leg</u>, torso, and arms are in one line.

Measure 45: Step right back along left diagonal, left <u>leg</u> front <u>on pique</u>. Raise arms to front horizontal, elbows leading.

Measure 46: Step left back along left diagonal, right <u>leg</u> front <u>on pique</u>, lower arms to body, elbows leading and continue to left low. Turn head right to look toward audience.

Measure 47:

> Counts 1–2: Shift weight of body front to right <u>lunge,</u> and with swing of right arm to side, turn ninety degrees to right on right <u>demi-plié</u> to **face right diagonal**. Left leg describes circle along floor, finishing with left <u>leg</u> front <u>on pique</u>. During turn, <u>dorsal side bend</u> left, left arm side.

> Count 3: Shift weight front to left leg, right <u>leg</u> back <u>on pique</u>. Straighten torso, left arm side low, right <u>arm wave</u>, finishing both arms side low.

Measure 48: Through <u>demi-plié</u> on left, <u>arabesque</u> on left, body slightly tilted forward, <u>arm waves</u> front, arms <u>parallel</u>.

Measure 49: Step back on right and cross left over right. Lower arms to body.

Measure 50: Turn 270 degrees to right in <u>relevé</u> to **face left diagonal**. Finish standing on left, right <u>parallel</u> bent front on ball of foot, arms close to body.

Measure 51: Repeat movement of measure 47, counts 1–2 (turn in <u>demi-plié</u>), expanding movement of 2 counts to 3 counts. At the end of this measure, dancers **face right diagonal**.

Measure 52: Shift weight of body front to left <u>lunge</u>, putting left hand below left hip, and repeat movement of measure 51 to opposite side.

> Change: During turn, right leg now describes circle low above floor and right arm mirrors movement of right leg, turning right elbow outward, wrist leading. Turn additional 135 degrees to finish with **back to audience**. During this additional turn, lower right leg close to left to finish in <u>first (I) position</u>, both arms close to body.

Measures 53-83: Repeat movement of measures 5-35. Finish *facing audience*.

Note: Movement of measure 83 includes all movements in both measures 35 and 36.

Measure 84: Move arms down through sides to side low, legs from <u>relevé</u> to stand on left, bend turned out right behind left, ball of foot touching floor.

Portraits

Did you ever watch a portrait artist at a public forum and marvel at the multiple variations and interpretations of the people the artist sees?

Portraits

Dancing For Fun
Book 2

With Feeling

Mark L. Greathouse

Dance 5: Portraits Choreography

Key Signature: 4/4

Introduction: 4 notes

Starting formation: Two columns facing each other two arm lengths apart (column equals file perpendicular to audience, one dancer behind the next).

Starting position:

> **Odd-numbered dancers** on left side: standing on right leg with *left shoulder to audience*, left <u>leg</u> stretched back <u>on pique</u>, arms side low.

> **Even-numbered dancers** on right side: standing on left leg with *right shoulder to audience*, right <u>leg</u> stretched back <u>on pique</u>, arms side low.

> Note: Each column performs **mirror image** of the other in measures 1–12. Therefore only the movement of odd-numbered dancers is described.

Odd-numbered dancers in measures 1–12:

Measure 1: Close left to right to <u>parallel demi-plié.</u> <u>Windmill arms</u> right in <u>canon</u>. Dancer number one begins on count 1, dancer number three begins on count 2, dancer number five begins on count 3, dancer number seven begins on count 4.

Measure 2: All dancers simultaneously: starting in <u>parallel demi-plié</u>, start <u>windmill arms</u> left; at highest point turn 180 degrees to left in <u>relevé</u>, finishing with *right shoulder to audience*, arms close to body.

> Note: **The two columns of dancers now with backs to each other.**

Measure 3:

> Counts 1–2: Step left front and <u>fouette</u> turn left (180 degrees). Swing both arms forward to high in <u>sagittal plane</u>. Finish with *left shoulder toward audience*.

Counts 3-4: Step right back and through bending both knees and shifting weight to right, finish standing on right, left leg front on pique. Lower arms to body through front. During stretching of knees, slide hands along body from down to up, bending elbows, finally stretching arms overhead. Torso leans backward so that left leg, torso, arms, and head are in one line.

Measures 4-5: Two chaines with dorsal side bends turning to left, moving parallel to audience.

Measure 6: Stand on left with **left shoulder to audience**, right stretched back, ball of foot touching floor, arms close to body.

Measure 7:

Counts 1-2: Step right front.

Counts 3-4: Turning ninety degrees to right with **back to audience**, step left front (away from audience).

Measure 8: Turning forty-five degrees to right on **right back diagonal**, step on right relevé and turn 135 degrees to right in left low arabesque. During arabesque turn, right arm front high, left back low. Finish in first (I) position **facing audience**, arms close to body.

Measure 9:

Counts 1-2: Moving both arms to left in frontal plane, start windmill arms right through relevé.

Counts 3-4: Step left front to demi-plié on left. Bend right leg behind left (away from left foot), touching floor with ball of foot. Finish windmill arms to right into dorsal side bend to right.

Measure 10: Straighten left knee, and with slight push from right leg, turn 360 degrees to right on left, gradually closing straight right leg to left, finishing in first (I) position **facing audience**, arms close to body.

Measure 11:

Counts 1-2: Moving both arms to right in frontal plane, start windmill arms left through relevé.

Counts 3–4: Step left front to <u>demi-plié</u> on left. Bend right leg behind left (away from left foot), touching floor with ball of foot. Finish <u>windmill arms</u> to left into <u>dorsal side bend</u> to left.

Measure 12:

Counts 1–2: Straighten body and both legs, keeping legs stationary with weight on left. Open arms to sides slightly higher than horizontal, head and chest up.

Counts 3–4: Bend legs to reach same position as in measure 11, counts 3–4. Through <u>dorsal backbend</u>, lower body gradually to finish in <u>dorsal front bend</u>, arms vertical in front of body.

Note: In measures 13–14 movement is done in <u>canon</u>.

Note: <u>Canon</u> is as follows: couple one moves, followed by couple two, followed by couple three, etc.

Measure 13:

Count 1: **First couple** (dancers one and two):

Odd-numbered dancer turns ninety degrees to right with ***left shoulder to audience***, closing right leg to left into <u>first (I) position</u>; right arm moves first front and then in <u>horizontal plane</u> to side horizontal.

Even-numbered dancer turns ninety degrees to left with ***right shoulder to audience***, closing left leg to right into <u>first (I) position</u>; left arm moves first front and then in <u>horizontal plane</u> to side horizontal.

Other couples remain in place.

Count 2: **Second couple** (dancers three and four) same as dancers one and two in count 1. Other couples remain in place.

Count 3: **Third couple** (dancers five and six) same as dancers one and two in count 1. Other couples remain in place.

Count 4: **Fourth couple** (dancers seven and eight) same as dancers one and two in count 1. Other couples remain in place.

Note: Movement of working arm (right arm for odd-numbered dancers and left arm for even-numbered dancers) is slow and continuous, even when leg movement is not.

Note: Measure 14 is done in <u>canon</u> in reverse order.

Measure 14:

Count 1: **Fourth couple** (dancers seven and eight):

Odd-numbered dancer crosses left leg over right and turns 270 degrees to right, finishing in <u>first (I) position</u> *facing audience*, arms close to body.

Even-numbered dancer crosses right leg over left and turns 270 degrees to left, finishing in <u>first (I) position</u> *facing audience*, arms close to body.

Other couples remain in place.

Count 2: **Third couple** (dancers five and six) same as dancers seven and eight in count 1. Other couples remain in place.

Count 3: **Second couple** (dancers three and four) same as dancers seven and eight in count 1. Other couples remain in place.

Count 4: **First couple** (dancers one and two) same as dancers seven and eight in count 1. Other couples remain in place.

Note: Each column performs **mirror image** of the other in measure 15. Therefore only the movement of odd-numbered dancers is described.

Odd-numbered dancers in measure 15:

Measure 15:

Counts 1–2: Turning ninety degrees to left with *right shoulder to audience*, <u>lunge</u> on left, left arm low front, right arm low back. Subsequently turn ninety degrees to left, finishing with **back to audience** on left <u>demi-plié</u>, right foot making arc on floor, finishing <u>leg</u> side <u>on pique</u>.

Counts 3-4: Cross right leg over left and turn 180 degrees to left in <u>relevé</u>, arms close to body, finishing in <u>first (I) position</u> **facing audience**.

Note: In measure 16 dancers dissolve columns and move into **staggered rows**.

Note: In measures 16-26 dancers perform **in unison**.

Measure 16: Run to finish **facing audience** in **staggered lines** in <u>first (I) position</u>, arms close to body.

Measure 17: <u>Windmill arms</u> right.

Measure 18: <u>Windmill arms</u> left, turning ninety degrees left with **right shoulder to audience**. At end of measure, arms are close to body.

Note: In measures 19-22 all dancers move in unison (as written in text). That means if there is a reference to previous measures, then all dancers do movements of **odd-numbered dancers**.

Measures 19-22: Repeat movement of measures 3-6 (<u>fouette</u> turn, <u>chaines with dorsal side bends</u>), finishing with **left shoulder to audience**.

Measures 23-24: Take three steps (right, left, right) and close left to right into <u>first (I) position</u>, arms close to body. By the end of measure 24 dancers have formed one single-file **facing audience**. Ideally, finish so that the shortest dancers are in front and tallest are in back.

Measure 25: In <u>canon</u> move both arms back low, elbows leading, and then turn arms with wrists leading to cross arms in front of body; execute <u>dorsal front bend</u>, head down. First dancer in column bends the lowest and can bend legs to <u>plié</u>; last dancer need not bend knees at all and just does movement of arms and body. Left leg on ball of foot, and consequently left knee is higher than right.

Measure 26: Gradually straighten body, one vertebra at a time, finishing standing in <u>first (I) position</u> **facing audience**.

Note: From measure 27 to the end of the dance, **odd-numbered and even-numbered dancers** perform in **mirror image** of the other. Therefore only the movement of odd-numbered dancers is described.

Odd-numbered dancers:

Measure 27: <u>Dorsal side bend</u> to right, stretching right arm side and then high while straightening torso. Prepare left <u>leg on pique</u> left side. Subsequently turn ninety degrees to left with *right shoulder to audience*. Kneel on right, sit on right heel, left leg bent front with foot on floor close to right knee. Sharp bend at left knee, palms on floor close to body; head down close to left knee.

Note: Dancers are now in **two columns with back to each other**.

Measure 28: Sit on right hip, turn ninety degrees to left with *back to audience*, knees together, bent at sharp angle, toes touching floor; embrace knees with head down to knees. Turn 180 degrees to left to *face audience*, kneeling on both knees and sitting on heels, head to knees, arms close to body.

Measure 29: Rise on knees. With both arms parallel to each other, make full circle to right in <u>frontal plane</u> (right side up, left side down). Continue circle to right low. Head follows arm movements.

Measure 30:

Counts 1-2: Slide body to right side to lie on floor, right arm stretched on floor; head rests on right arm, left arm on palm in front of chest, elbow bent, forearm vertical. Bend both legs: right leg in right angle, angle of left leg greater than right angle.

Counts 3-4: Pushing from left arm, raise body to vertical to sit on right hip; *face audience*. Keeping right leg stationary, slide bent left leg along floor to back, arms side low, fingers touching body, head up.

Measure 31:

Counts 1-2: With impulse, rise from right hip to both knees and turn forty-five degrees left to *face left diagonal*, kneeling on right knee, left leg ninety degrees bent front, flat foot on floor, right arm front, left arm side.

Counts 3-4: Rise to <u>lunge</u> on left and with impulse turn 405 degrees (one and an eighth circles) to right on left <u>relevé</u>, closing straight right leg to left, arms close to body to finish in <u>first (I) position</u> **facing audience**.

Note: During measure 32, left arm is always close to body.

Measure 32:

Counts 1-2: <u>Parallel demi-plié</u>, right arm to side, head follows right arm, <u>dorsal side bend</u> to right, <u>relevé</u> on both feet, right arm circle right side up to overhead (start circle in <u>frontal plane</u>). Turn ninety degrees to left, finishing with **right shoulder to audience**.

Counts 3-4: Raise stretched left leg low front and step left front, right <u>leg</u> back <u>on pique</u>. Right arm finishes circle (now in <u>sagittal plane</u>) from up through front to down.

Note: During measure 33, left arm is always close to body.

Measure 33:

Counts 1-2: Step right and cross left over right.

Counts 3-4: Turn 360 degrees to right on <u>relevé</u> on both feet. Both arms close to body.

Measure 34: Stepping right side to <u>lunge</u>, continue with two <u>chaines</u> to right toward audience. Keep arms close to body, and in last movement slight arc with right arm low, front to side. Finish **facing audience**.

Measure 35: Step left front and then turn ninety degrees to left (now with **right shoulder to audience**) and step right front, arms close to body.

Measure 36:

Counts 1-2: Turn ninety degrees to left with **back to audience**. Step left front away from audience and close right leg to left, right <u>parallel</u> bent front, touching floor on ball of foot.

Counts 3-4: Turning 180 degrees to left on <u>relevé</u> on both feet, finish **facing audience** in <u>first (I) position</u>. Arms remain close to body.

Measure 37: <u>Windmill arms</u> right while turning ninety degrees to right with **left shoulder to audience**. Finish in <u>parallel</u> <u>demi-plié</u>, <u>dorsal side bend</u> to right.

Measure 38: <u>Windmill arms</u> left while turning ninety degrees to left to finish **facing audience** in <u>demi-plié</u> on left, right leg bent, ball of right foot touching floor behind left, <u>dorsal side bend</u> to left.

Measure 39:

> Counts 1–2: Step right side with side bend to left, right arm side high, head follows movement of right arm, close left leg to right, left leg bent, ball of left foot touching floor behind right.

> Counts 3–4: Cross left leg over right and turn 360 degrees to right on <u>relevé</u> to **face audience**, arms close to body.

Measure 40:

> Counts 1–2: Lower heels from <u>relevé</u> to stand on both legs and continue to <u>parallel demi-plié</u> on both. Start circle in <u>frontal plane</u> with left arm moving down, to right, and then up; head follows left arm.

> Counts 3–4: Turn ninety degrees to left with **right shoulder to audience**, step left front, continue circle with left down (now in <u>sagittal plane</u>), and start circle with right back and then up in <u>sagittal plane</u>. Close right leg to left on ball of foot, <u>parallel</u> bent. Finish circle with right arm down.

> Note: It is important that arms follow each other (right chases the left, 180 degrees behind the left). Movement is continuous.

Measure 41: Cross right over left and turn 360 degrees to left on <u>relevé</u>, arms close to body. At end of turn, swing right arm to left in front of body in <u>horizontal plane</u>.

Measure 42:

> Counts 1–2: Step right back to <u>lunge</u> back on right. Stretched left leg touching floor with heel, foot flexed. During stepping right back, bend right elbow, and move right arm to front horizontal, palm up. Then swing right arm in <u>sagittal plane</u> back, turn torso to right toward audience. Left arm swings to right in

frontal plane following right arm swing back. Dorsal side bend to left; head to right.

Counts 3-4: Shift weight to left front and turn on flat left foot 270 degrees to left. During turn, both knees touch each other, right lower leg back horizontal. Arms close to body. Finish in first (I) position **facing audience**.

Measure 43:

Counts 1-2: Pushing right hip out, execute long and slow chassé step right along right diagonal, both legs bent. At start of chassé step, put right arm side and left arm front horizontal. At close of chassé step, slightly lower arms in same position. Head to right.

Counts 3-4: Repeat movement of counts 1-2.

Measure 44: Repeat movement of previous measure along left diagonal to opposite side.

Measure 45:

Counts 1-2: Turn body to **face audience**. Taking off from left, jump onto right sideways, both legs straight in the air, and land on right demi-plié, left crossed behind right in frontal plane stretched to right as far as possible, touching floor with ball of left foot. Arms are front low with palms up; during jump, turn hands inward, finishing with "reversed" palms up (twisted wrists). During landing, right arm side low and left arm parallel with right in frontal plane low.

Counts 3-4: Closing left leg to right, turn 360 degrees to left to **face audience** in parallel first (I) position. Shift weight of body to right leg. Arms close to body.

Measure 46:

Counts 1-2: Through slight demi-plié on right, take off from right, land on left (movement done in place), subsequently parallel develope with right leg to back, finishing in lunge on left, right leg back on pique. Arms are front low; during jump, starting with palms up, turn hands inward, palms up, finishing with left arm low side, right arm low front. Lean forward so that torso and right leg are in one line.

Counts 3–4: Turn 180 degrees to right with **back to audience**. Stepping on right relevé, slide stretched left leg to right, turning another 180 degrees to right on relevé. Finish **facing audience** in first (I) position. Close arms to body.

Measure 47:

Counts 1–2: Repeat movement of counts 1–2 of measure 43 (long chassé step right), but move to right **facing audience**.

Counts 3–4: Repeat movement of counts 1–2 of measure 44 (long chassé step left), but move to left **facing audience**.

Measure 48:

Counts 1–2: Step right to side and cross left leg over right, close arms to body.

Counts 3–4: Turn 270 degrees on relevé on both feet to right. Finish with **right shoulder to audience** standing on left, right leg parallel bent, ball of foot touching floor, one foot-length in front of left leg. Arms close to body.

Measures 49–52: Repeat movement of measures 41–44 (lunge back, long chassé steps).

Measure 53:

Counts 1–2: Repeat movement of measure 45, counts 1–2 (jump onto right sideways).

Counts 3–4: Closing left leg to right, turn 270 degrees to left, finishing with **left shoulder to audience** in parallel first (I) position. Arms close to body.

Measure 54:

Counts 1–2: Through slight demi-plié on left, take off from left, land on right (movement done in place), and subsequently parallel develope with left leg to front, finishing in lunge back on right, left leg front on pique. Arms are front low. During jump, starting with palms up, turn hands inward, palms up, finishing with left arm low side, right arm low front. Lean back so that torso and left leg are in one line.

Counts 3–4: Shift weight front onto left leg and turn 270 degrees to right, closing right leg to left, to finish **facing audience** in first (I) position. Close arms to body.

Measure 55: Repeat movement of measure 47 to opposite side (long chassé steps left and right).

Measure 56:

Counts 1–2: Step left side and cross right leg over left; close arms to body.

Counts 3–4: Turn 270 degrees to left in relevé on both feet. Finish with **left shoulder to audience** standing on right, left leg parallel bent, ball of foot touching floor, one foot-length in front of right leg. Turn torso to left to face audience, left arm side low, right arm touching body in front low, bent at elbow, forearm parallel with left arm.

Clown Dance

Clowns make us laugh, but don't they actually

portray a perspective on reality?

Can they teach us something about life?

Clown Dance

Allegro

Mark L. Greathouse

Piano

Dance 6: Clown Dance Choreography

Key Signature: 3/4

Introduction: 4 measures

Starting formation: Dancers are in one column (single file in middle of dance floor).

Odd-numbered dancers with **_right shoulder to audience_**.

Even-numbered dancers with **_left shoulder to audience_**.

Starting position: Standing in first (I) position, each dancer with arms down behind body, right hand in left, resting on lower back.

> Note: In measures 1-4 movement is in canon, assuming six dancers. At the end of measure 4, dancers are in **V formation** with dancers one and two at the point of the "V" closest to audience. Therefore dancers one and two run the shortest distance; dancers five and six run the longest distance.

> Note: During measures 1-12, arms remain behind body as in starting position.

Measure 1: Hold starting position.

Measure 2: Dancers one and two turn slightly toward middle of dance floor and run forward, away from each other, in approximately diagonal direction. At the end of run, finish **_facing audience_**. All other dancers remain in place.

Measure 3: Dancers three and four move as dancers one and two in previous measure but for longer distance. All other dancers remain in place.

Measure 4: Dancers five and six move as dancers three and four in previous measure but for still longer distance. All other dancers remain in place.

Note: Each side of V formation performs **mirror image** of the other in measures 5–20. Therefore only the movement of odd-numbered dancers is described.

Odd-numbered dancers in measures 5–20:

Measure 5: Step side left, lift right leg to front <u>attitude</u>, <u>dorsal side bend</u> to right. Look toward left at right foot.

Measure 6: Same as movement in measure 5 but to opposite side. Dancers still face audience.

Measures 7–8: Step side left, and closing stretched right leg to left, turn 270 degrees to left on <u>relevé</u>, finishing in <u>first (I) position</u> with **left shoulder to audience**.

Measures 9–12: Repeat movement of measures 5–8 with following change:

> Change: Last turn in measure 12 is 450 degrees (one and a quarter circles) to finish **facing audience**.

Measure 13: Step side left to <u>demi-plié</u> on left and shift left hip toward audience. Keep stretched right leg stationary, flexing right foot, and touching floor with right heel. <u>Arms in frontal plane</u> to left, side bend to right; look over right shoulder at even-numbered partner.

Measure 14: Shift weight to right to stand on right. Through sliding, close left leg to right and bend left knee parallel forward, ball of left foot touching floor. Side bend to left, <u>arms in frontal plane</u> to right; head follows right arm. (Because of side bend, direction of arms will be nearly vertical.)

Measure 15: Repeat movement of measure 13 ("bowing").

Measure 16: With slight push from left leg, shift weight to right and then close left leg to right at knee (thighs are together down to knees), left leg back in right angle. Turn on right flat foot 360 degrees to right to finish in <u>first (I) position</u> **facing audience**. Swing arms to right low and then close them to body.

Measure 17:

> Count 1: Step side right on <u>relevé</u>, right arm side to horizontal; bend right elbow at right angle, forearm horizontal, palm down.

> Count 2: Repeat movement of count 1 to opposite side (<u>second (II) position relevé</u> at the end of count 2.)

Count 3: Move right leg toward left leg, finishing on right <u>relevé</u>, but not touching left foot. Keeping right elbow stationary, rotate right forearm outward in <u>frontal plane</u> to maximum and then lower entire arm close to body, keeping palm turned away from body.

Measure 18:

Count 1: Repeat movement of count 3 of measure 17 to opposite side, now finishing in <u>first (I) position</u> <u>relevé</u>.

Counts 2-3: Lower heels to stand in <u>first (I) position</u>. Arms remain close to body.

Measure 19: Turning ninety degrees to right with **left shoulder to audience**, repeat leg movements of measure 17.

Change: In counts 1-2 add additional movement to arms such that from forearm horizontal, with elbow leading to side up, stretch arm to side high. In count 3: through bending right elbow side down, close right arm to body.

Measure 20:

Count 1: Legs: repeat movement of count 1, measure 18.

Arms: repeat movement of count 3 of measure 19 to opposite side.

Counts 2-3: Lower heels to stand in <u>first (I) position</u>. Arms remain close to body.

Note: Diagonal lines of dancers are now **facing each other**.

Odd-numbered dancers in measures 21-23.

Measure 21: Turning forty-five degrees to left to **face right diagonal**, left <u>lunge</u>. Put one hand on the other on thigh just above left knee, slightly bending elbows; keep torso vertical and swing right leg to back <u>attitude</u>.

Measure 22: Lower right leg to touch floor behind body with ball of foot; hold <u>lunge</u> on left.

Measure 23: Repeat movement of measure 21 without initial turn.

Even-numbered dancers in measures 21-23.

Measure 21: Hold position from last measure.

Measure 22: Turning forty-five degrees to right to **face left diagonal**, right <u>lunge</u>. Put one hand on the other on thigh just above right knee, slightly bending elbows; keep torso vertical and swing left leg to back <u>attitude</u>.

Measure 23: Lower left leg to touch floor behind body with ball of foot; hold <u>lunge</u> on right.

> Note: Each side of V formation performs **mirror image** of the other in measure 24. Therefore only the movement of odd-numbered dancers is described.

Odd-numbered dancers in measure 24:

Measure 24: Step back on right, cross left over right, and turn 315 degrees to right on <u>relevé</u> to finish in <u>first (I) position</u> **facing audience**. Swing both arms in <u>horizontal plane</u> low away from each other, finishing behind back as in initial position.

> Note: In measures 25–32 all dancers do same movements in unison (as written in text). That means if there is a reference to previous measures, then all dancers do movements of **odd-numbered dancers**.

Measures 25–28: Repeat movement of measures 5–8 (lifts to front <u>attitude</u> and turn).

Measure 29: Repeat movement of measure 6 (left front <u>attitude</u>).

Measure 30: Repeat movement of measure 5 (right front <u>attitude</u>).

Measures 31–32: Step side right, and while closing stretched left leg to right leg, turn 270 degrees to right on <u>relevé</u> to finish in <u>first (I) position</u> **facing audience**.

> Note: From measure 33 to measure 38 dancers are divided into **odd-numbered and even-numbered dancers** and move in **mirror image**. Therefore only the movement of odd-numbered dancers is described.

> Note: From measure 33 to measure 36 dancers perform in <u>canon</u> so that **odd-numbered dancers** perform first and **even-numbered dancers** perform after them.

Odd-numbered dancers:

Measures 33–34: Step left side and <u>cartwheel</u> left.

Note: If dancers cannot do <u>cartwheel</u> left, take additional step with right and <u>cartwheel</u> to right. If dancers cannot do <u>cartwheel</u> at all, <u>chaines with dorsal side bends</u> to left, moving parallel to audience, away from center of dance floor.

In any case, finish with **_right shoulder to audience_**, kneeling on right knee, sitting on right heel, left leg bent at sharp angle, left flat foot on floor close to right thigh, head down, palms on floor at sides of body.

Note: It is advisable that the first dancer in each column do a <u>cartwheel</u>. The remaining dancers perform as they are able.

Measures 35-36: Hold position from previous measure.

Measures 37-38: Sit on right hip and then turn ninety degrees to left with **_back to audience_** to sit with legs bent and together, arms embracing knees, head to knees, toes pointed.

Even-numbered dancers:

Measures 33-34: Hold position from previous measure.

Measures 35-36: Execute movement of **odd-numbered dancers** from measures 33-34 to opposite side.

Measures 37-38: Sit on left hip and then turn ninety degrees to right with **_back to audience_** to sit with legs bent and together, arms embracing knees, head to knees, toes pointed.

Note: In measures 39-46, dancers perform **in unison**.

Measures 39-40: Roll back to be supported on floor by head and shoulders in <u>shoulder stand</u>. Place hands on small of back to support hips.

Measures 41-42: Bend right leg at sharp angle and place behind left thigh. With impulse forward through sitting on right hip, rise on right knee, left leg bent forward to right angle, flat foot on floor, and continue rising onto left leg, right <u>leg</u> back <u>on pique</u>, arms close to body.

Measures 43-44: Cross right leg over left and turn 180 degrees to left in <u>relevé</u> to finish **_facing audience_** in <u>first (I) position</u>.

Note: In measures 45-52 dancers form **one column** in middle of dance floor, **_facing audience_**. In order to achieve this formation, some dancers must move forward, some to the side and some diagonally. Arms remain close to body.

Measure 45: Step left front.

Measure 46: Step right front.

Measures 47-48: Cross left leg over right and turn 360 degrees to right in relevé to finish *facing audience*.

Measures 49-52: Repeat movement of measures 45-48 (steps and turn).

Note: In measures 53 through 68 dancers are again divided into **odd-numbered** and **even-numbered dancers**. Movements are done in **mirror image**. Therefore only the movement of odd-numbered dancers is described.

Note: In measures 53-54 movement is done in canon.

Note: Canon is as follows: dancer one moves, followed by dancer two, followed by dancer three, etc.

Measures 53-54:

Odd-numbered dancers cross left leg over right and turn 360 degrees to right to *face audience*.

Even-numbered dancers do this in opposite fashion.

Note: Everyone moves away from middle of dance floor in line parallel with audience. At the end, dancers are in **two columns** *facing audience*.

Odd-numbered dancers in measures 55-56:

Measure 55: Arms in frontal plane to left.

Measure 56: Step right side to side lunge on right; simultaneously move arms down in frontal plane to right. Stretch body to right, head looks at right arm, right arm higher than horizontal.

Note: In measures 57-58 movement is done in canon.

Note: Canon is as follows: dancer one moves, followed by dancer two, followed by dancer three, etc.

Measures 57-58:

Odd-numbered dancers cross right leg over left and turn 360 degrees to left to *face audience*.

Even-numbered dancers do this in opposite fashion.

Note: Everyone moves toward the middle of dance floor in line parallel with audience. At the end dancers are in **one column** *facing audience*.

Measures 59-60: Repeat movement of measures 55-56 (side <u>lunge</u>).

Odd-numbered dancers in measures 61-64:

Measure 61: Cross left leg over right and turn 270 degrees to right, **right shoulder to audience**, arms close to body.

Note: At end of measure 61 dancers are in **two columns** *facing each other*.

Measure 62: Step right back on <u>relevé</u>. Rotate arms so that palms face forward and then move arms back in <u>sagittal plane</u>, elbows leading, arms move very close to body. Stretch left leg front to horizontal and continue arm movement with elbows leading, now reversing direction and moving forward until arms are stretched front horizontal, palms down, and turned outward with thumbs down.

Measure 63:

Count 1: Step left back on <u>relevé</u>, arms low front.

Counts 2-3: Turning forty-five degrees to right, step right to right side <u>lunge</u> **along right diagonal**. Raise left arm to side, right arm circles in <u>frontal plane</u> to left, up, and to right, finishing right side horizontal with palm up. Head follows right arm and body stretches to right at end of measure.

Measure 64: Shift weight to left, and crossing right leg over left, turn 405 degrees (one and an eighth circles) to left to *face audience* in <u>first (I) position</u> <u>relevé</u>. Arms close to body.

Note: Measures 65-66 in <u>canon</u>: first **odd-numbered** and then **even-numbered dancers**.

Measure 65: **Odd-numbered dancers**:

Count 1: Turning forty-five degrees to right to *face right diagonal*, step left front. Put left hand on left thigh below hip.

Count 2: Demi-plié on left and subsequently straighten left knee. Parallel developé with right to horizontal (or higher). Right arm makes big circle backward in sagittal plane. Look up.

Count 3: Step on right and close left leg to right to stand on right, left parallel bent front, ball of left foot touching floor next to right foot. Right arm finishes circle. At end, right hand touches left hand on left side of body.

Even-numbered dancers hold position from previous measure.

Measure 66:

Even-numbered dancers are doing movement of odd-numbered dancers from measure 65 but in **mirror image**.

Odd-numbered dancers hold position from previous measure.

Odd-numbered dancers in measures 67–68:

Measure 67: Cross left leg over right and turn 315 degrees in relevé to right to *face audience*, arms close to body.

Measure 68: Long side lunge to left, arms side low, and then closing stretched right leg to left, turn 360 degrees to left to *face audience*.

Note: at the end of measure 68, dancers are in **one column** *facing audience*.

Measures 69–84: Same movement as in measures 53–68.

Note: In measures 85–86 dancers form **two columns** and maintain them until measure 98.

Measure 85:

Odd-numbered dancers: Repeat movement of measure 13 ("bowing").

Even-numbered dancers: Hold position from previous measure.

Measure 86:

> **Odd-numbered dancers**: Hold position from previous measure.

> **Even-numbered dancers**: Repeat movement of odd-numbered dancers from previous measure to opposite side.

> Note: Measures 87-90: movement for **odd-numbered dancers** will be described below. **Even-numbered dancers** perform in **mirror image**. Therefore only the movement of odd-numbered dancers is described.

Odd-numbered dancers:

Measures 87-89: Repeat movement of measures 14-16 ("bowing" and turn).

Measure 90: Turning ninety degrees to left with *right shoulder to audience*, step to left lunge, left arm front low, right arm back low. Turn 270 degrees to left, closing stretched right leg to left. Finish in first (I) position *facing audience*, close arms to body.

> Note: In measures 91-95 dancers move **in unison**.

Measure 91: Repeat measure 19 without initial turn (steps in relevé with arm movements.) Dancers now *face audience*.

Measure 92: Parallel demi-plié, dorsal front bend, arms down.

Measures 93-95: Repeat movement of measures 62-64 (steps back on relevé, side lunge, and turn) with change.

> Change: First step in measure 94 is done with ninety-degree turn to left so that after this step dancers have *right shoulder to audience*.

> Note: In measures 96-98 dancers are divided into **odd- and even-numbered dancers** and perform in **mirror image**. Therefore only the movement of odd-numbered dancers is described.

Odd-numbered dancers:

Measure 96: Step left side and cartwheel left.

> Note: If dancers cannot do cartwheel left, take additional step with right and cartwheel to right. If dancers cannot do cartwheel at all, chaines with

dorsal side bends to left, moving parallel to audience, away from center of dance floor.

In any case, finish standing on left with **right shoulder to audience**.

> Note: It is advisable that the first dancer in each column does cartwheel.

> Note: Dancers are moving from middle outward.

Measures 97-98: Relevé on left, right leg lifted back low, followed by runs along arc of 270 degrees to left. Finish **facing audience** in **staggered lines**.

> Note: In measures 99-110 dancers move **in unison**.

Measures 99-110: Repeat movement of measures 5-16 (all dancers do same movements in unison as written in text. That means if there is a reference to previous measures, then all dancers do movements of **odd-numbered dancers**).

> Note: Measures 111-114 in canon. First row of dancers performs in measures 111-112. All other rows perform in measures 113-114.

Measures 111-112: **First row**: step left side and cartwheel left.

> Note: If dancers cannot do cartwheel left, take additional step with right and cartwheel to right. If dancers cannot do cartwheel at all, chaines with dorsal side bends to left, moving parallel to audience, away from center of dance floor. However, it is advisable that this first row performs cartwheel.

In any case, finish with **right shoulder to audience**, kneeling on right knee, sitting on right heel, left leg bent at sharp angle, left flat foot on floor close to right thigh, head down, palms on floor at sides of body.

Other rows: Hold position from previous measure.

Measures 113-114: **All other rows**: chaines with dorsal side bends to left, moving parallel to audience. It is also possible to perform cartwheel. However, everybody in these rows must do same movement.

In any case, finish with **right shoulder to audience**, kneeling on right knee, sitting on right heel, left leg bent at sharp angle, left flat foot on floor close to right thigh, head down, palms on floor at sides of body.

First row: Hold position from previous measure.

Measures 115–122: Repeat movement of measures 37–44 (<u>shoulder stand</u> and turn).

> Note: In measures 123–128 dancers form **one column** in middle of dance floor, *facing audience*. In order to achieve this formation, some dancers must move forward, some to the side, and some diagonally. Arms remain close to body.

Measure 123: Step left front.

Measure 124: Step right front.

Measures 125–126: Cross left leg over right and turn 360 degrees to right to *face audience* in <u>first (I) position</u>. During turn, right arm moves away from body slightly, elbow leading; turn palm up, arm moves from front to side and then close to body.

Measures 127–128: Repeat movement of 123–124 (steps).

> Note: Dancers are now in **one column**.

Measure 129: Cross left leg over right and turn 360 degrees to right to *face audience* in <u>first (I) position</u> relevé. During turn raise both arms through front to <u>third position of arms</u>.

> Note: In measure 130 dancers are divided into **odd- and even-numbered dancers** and perform in **mirror image**. Therefore only the movement of odd-numbered dancers is described.

Movement of **odd-numbered dancers**:

Measure 130: Take long step with right leg across left (in <u>frontal plane</u> to left side) with side bend to right. Circle both arms in <u>frontal plane</u> to right, down, and to left; continue overhead to right and then down and to left. Arms describe circle in continuous movement in <u>frontal plane</u>. Lower body to kneel on left knee, right bent front. Move to left hip, lie down, left leg bent on floor and right leg stretched over left leg, toes pointed, left arm stretched with head resting on left arm, right arm bent in front of body with palm on floor. Entire body in one line, parallel with audience.

Remembrance

We all have memories of calm, peaceful

periods in our lives as well as of

exciting, eventful times.

Remembrance

Dancing For Fun
Book 2

Mark L. Greathouse

Slowly, with Feeling

Dance 7: Remembrance Choreography

Key signature: 3/4 changes to 4/4 beginning with measure 33

Introduction: 3 initial notes

Starting formation: Dancers in **staggered rows**.

Starting position (with first 3 notes): Stand on right with ***back to audience***, left <u>leg</u> back <u>on pique</u>. Arms close to sides. Head down.

Measure 1: Shifting weight back to left, bend left knee and straighten to stand on left, right <u>leg</u> front <u>on pique</u>. Raise left arm to side; head follows movement of arm.

Measure 2: Step right back and repeat movement of measure 1 to opposite side.

> Note: In measures 1–2 arm and leg movements occur simultaneously on same side.

Measure 3: Step left back and repeat leg movement from measure 1. Lower arms to body and immediately raise them up sideways to <u>third position of arms</u> overhead.

Measure 4: Slide stretched right leg to left into <u>fifth (V) position</u> <u>relevé</u>, right leg front; <u>soutenu turn</u> 180 degrees to left, finishing to ***face audience***. Step immediately left forward toward audience through <u>demi-plié</u> and straighten to stand on left, right <u>leg</u> back <u>on pique</u>. During turn, maintain <u>third position of arms</u>. During step, open arms to sides and gradually lower them to close to body.

Measures 5–8: Repeat leg movements of measures 1–4 to opposite side (now start with right leg, movement away from audience).

> Change: Last <u>soutenu turn</u> is modified to be 360 degrees to finish ***facing audience*** in <u>fifth (V) position</u> <u>relevé</u>, right leg front. During first step, left arm rises to side; during second step, right arm rises to side. Otherwise arm movement the same as in measures 1–4.

Note: In measures 5-6 arm and leg movements occur simultaneously on opposite sides.

Measure 9: Through <u>demi-plié</u> on left, turn forty-five degrees to right to **face right diagonal**. Step right front on <u>relevé</u> and turn 360 degrees on right to right, left leg in <u>parallel</u> <u>cou-de-pied</u>. Bend elbows and cross arms close to front of upper body.

Measure 10: Stretch left <u>leg</u> front <u>on pique</u> and slide forward along floor into <u>split</u> (or <u>partial split</u>) with stretched legs. Touch floor with left hand. <u>Dorsal side bend</u> to left, right arm side up so that both arms are in one line.

Measure 11: Sit on floor on left hip and bend both legs to approximately ninety degrees, left leg front, right leg back. Through <u>dorsal side bend</u> to right, give impulse with left hand from floor and turn on seat 225 degrees to left, finishing with **back to audience**. During turn, bring both bent legs together in front of body. <u>Dorsal bend</u> forward, head down; right arm holds both legs, knees together. At end of turn, cross right foot over left at ankle, toes pointed to floor to break rotation of turn. Forehead touches knees.

Measure 12: Stretch both legs along floor away from audience, torso vertical. Then touch floor with left hand, roll body 180 degrees to left, put right hand on floor, lower upper body to floor through <u>dorsal backbend</u>, keeping elbows bent and close to body. At the end of measure, dancers are lying on stomach, **head toward audience**, forehead touching floor.

Measure 13: Swinging stretched right leg back and up, push with left hand from floor. Leading with right shoulder, sit up while turning ninety degrees to right, finishing with **left shoulder to audience**. Sit on left hip, both legs bent approximately ninety degrees, left front, right back. <u>Dorsal backbend</u>, head up, both arms stretched back low, fingers touching floor.

Measure 14: Close right leg to left and through impulse rise on both knees, upper arms close to body, forearms crossed in <u>horizontal plane</u> in front of body, palms up.

Measure 15: Remain on right knee. Move left leg forward, flat foot on floor, left knee bent ninety degrees. Move arms through small circles inward, stretch right to front horizontal, left to side horizontal.

Measure 16: Rise with weight on left front. Close right leg to left to <u>relevé</u> and turn ninety degrees to right, finishing in <u>first (I) position</u> <u>relevé</u>, **back to audience**. By bending elbows to touch torso and keeping upper arms low, move forearms up, palms facing body, finishing with crossed arms, hands on opposite shoulders. Step front right, left <u>leg</u> back <u>on pique</u>. Open arms to horizontal V shape, palms up, and lower them to close to body.

Measures 17-24 (music repeats): Repeat movement of measures 1-8 as written. Modify the last <u>soutenu turn</u> in measure 24 as follows:

> Change: Turn 270 degrees to right finishing with **right shoulder to audience** in parallel <u>demi-plié</u>, knees together; continuous arm movement through sides to <u>third position of arms</u>. Lower arms in <u>sagittal plane</u> to left arm front, palm up, right arm back, palm up, twist torso to right. Continue arm movements to close arms to body.

Measure 25: Turn ninety degrees to right to **face audience**, and execute four mini-steps to right on <u>relevé</u> (step side right, close left to right—repeat four times). Continue movement of arms and upper body as follows: right arm to describe circle in <u>frontal plane</u>, left arm and upper body follow (right arm down; right arm to left, <u>dorsal side bend</u> to left, left arm to side; right arm up to overhead, straighten body; right arm to right side again and <u>dorsal side bend</u> to right, left arm up). Head follows movement of arms.

Measure 26: Repeat leg and arm movements of measure 25 to opposite side (omitting initial turn).

Measures 27-28: Turn forty-five degrees to right and repeat movement of measures 25 and 26 (omitting initial turn). Movement is now done **along back left diagonal**.

Measure 29: Repeat movement of measure 9 (turn in <u>parallel</u> <u>cou-de-pied</u>), omitting initial turn, i.e., movement is done along **right diagonal**.

Measure 30: Step left front through <u>demi-plié</u> on **right diagonal**. Through <u>develope</u> extend right leg front as high as possible, slightly twisting torso to left. Extended right leg and torso are in one line. Keep arms crossed and close to body.

Measure 31: Straighten body and take two steps (right, left) into <u>arabesque scale</u> on left <u>demi-plié</u>, right leg extended back to horizontal, torso horizontal; turn head to left. Parallel arms open during steps to front horizontal, palms up; continue close to body to rear during <u>arabesque scale</u>.

Measure 32: Turn 135 degrees to right with **back to audience** and take steps along half-circle arc to right (right, left and close right to left, right leg <u>bent parallel</u> front, ball of foot touching floor). Finish **facing audience**. Arms remain close to body during walk. At end of measure <u>dorsal side bend</u> to right, head turned to left; bend elbows and cross arms close to front of upper body.

Music theme changes.

Note: Music now has 4 counts per measure.

Measure 33:

Counts 1-2: Step side right and hop on right, left in <u>parallel</u> <u>cou-de-pied</u>, <u>dorsal side bend</u> to left. Straighten arms down; swing them parallel front and then cross them close to front of upper body, head turned left.

Counts 3-4: Step side left; slide bent right leg toward left, <u>dorsal side bend</u> to right, arms open to sides in one line, head turned left.

Measure 34: Turn ninety degrees to right (***left shoulder to audience***) and repeat movement of measure 33 with the following changes.

Change: First hop is done forward. Finish measure by crossing right leg over left and turning 180 degrees to left (***right shoulder to audience***), arms close to body.

Measure 35: Starting position of arms: right arm side to horizontal, palm up, left arm close to body. Execute 4 <u>chaines</u> to right toward audience as follows: turn 180 degrees to right with <u>dorsal side bend</u> toward stepping right leg; right arm lowers to close to body, elbow leading, palm up; left arm rises to horizontal, elbow leading, palm down. Repeat three more times changing sides.

Measure 36: Finish ***facing audience***, weight on straight left leg, right <u>leg</u> back <u>on pique</u>, <u>arms in frontal plane</u> to left, head turned to left.

Measures 37-40: Repeat movements of measures 33-36, but change some directions.

Changes:

In measure 37, counts 3-4: Step left back, turning ninety degrees to left (***right shoulder to audience***); look toward audience (head turned to right).

In measure 38:

Counts 1-2: Turn ninety degrees to right to ***face audience*** and hop forward.

Counts 3-4: Facing audience, step left side, <u>dorsal side bend</u> to right.

In measure 39: Turn ninety degrees to right with **left shoulder to audience**; <u>chaines</u> to right in line parallel to audience.

In measure 40: Finish in same position as at the end of measure 36 but standing on **right diagonal**.

Measure 41:

Note: Arm movements are continuous.

Count 1: Small jump through swinging right leg in <u>sagittal plane</u> (from back to front, brushing left leg, to right leg forty-five degrees front), taking off from left leg, landing on both feet in <u>fifth (V) position</u> <u>demi-plié</u>, right leg front. During this jump swing both arms parallel in <u>sagittal plane</u> to front horizontal and cross bent arms low in <u>frontal plane</u> close to body.

Count 2: Taking off from both feet, jump vertically with right leg toward floor, left leg in <u>arabesque</u>; movement in flight is forward. During jump, left arm back low, palm down, right arm front high, palm down.

Count 3: Land on right. Step left front on right diagonal and twist body to left to **face audience**. Right arm through bent elbow executes small circle in <u>frontal plane</u> behind head, starting inward down.

Count 4: Turn 180 degrees right on flat left foot to finish standing on left, right leg front <u>on pique</u>, facing **right back diagonal**. During turn, frontal circle with right arm close to body, inward down, finishing side low.

Measure 42: Turn forty-five degrees to right with **right shoulder to audience** and <u>chaines</u> to right parallel with audience, arms close to body, elbows slightly outward, fingers touching thighs. Finish standing on left, right <u>leg</u> back <u>on pique</u> facing **right back diagonal**.

Measure 43:

Counts 1-3: Through slight <u>demi-plié</u> on left and through swinging right leg in <u>sagittal plane</u> (from back to front, brushing left leg, to right leg forty-five degrees front), take off from left leg with small jump, turning in air 225 degrees to left. Close both legs together in air. Land on both feet in <u>fifth (V)</u>

position demi-plié, right leg front, **facing audience**. During jump, arms to sides. Finish with right arm front, left arm low back.

Count 4: Turn forty-five degrees to right and jump forward in **direction right diagonal**, taking off from both feet. Land in demi-plié on right, left stretched in low arabesque; left arm executes semi-circle from back to front, moving in horizontal plane, palm down. Head follows movement of left arm. Finish in first position of arms.

Measure 44: Step left front and small jump through swinging right leg in sagittal plane (from back to front, brushing left leg, to right leg forty-five degrees front). Taking off from left leg, close both legs together in air, turning forty-five degrees to left. Land on both feet in fifth (V) position demi-plié, right leg front, **facing audience**. During jump, raise right arm side up, head follows right arm, left arm side low.

Measure 45:

Counts 1-2: Turn forty-five degrees to right, step on right relevé toward **right diagonal** into low left arabesque. Twist torso to left and continue circle with right arm to left down and then to right. In the last moment twist torso to right to face right diagonal and through sagittal arc down and front, raise left arm so that arms are now parallel in front horizontal.

Counts 3-4: Demi-plié on right, keeping left leg in low arabesque. Turn head left to **face audience**; hold arms as in counts 1-2.

Measure 46:

Note: Movement is done parallel with audience, moving to left.

Turn forty-five degrees to left to **face audience** and step side left. Cross right leg over left, step side left, and taking off from left, jump turning 360 degrees in air to left, landing in demi-plié fifth (V) position, right leg front. During takeoff, swing right leg in frontal plane in front of left. During jump, close legs together. During side steps, both parallel arms move in frontal circle from right to down. During takeoff, swing arms to left; during jump, right arm continues high with fingers making horizontal circle overhead, left arm side low. After landing, lower right arm in frontal plane to side, palm up, left arm close to body; turn ninety degrees to left with **right shoulder toward audience**.

Measure 47: Repeat movement of measure 35 (4 <u>chaines</u> to right with <u>dorsal side bends</u> toward audience).

Measure 48:

>Counts 1–2: Finish standing on left **facing audience**, right <u>leg</u> back <u>on pique</u>, arms to left low in <u>frontal plane</u>.

>Count 3: Legs stationary, swing arms in <u>frontal plane</u> to right low.

>Count 4: Legs stationary, arms same as previous count but in opposite direction.

Music theme changes.

Measure 49:

>Counts 1–2: Turning forty-five degrees to left, step right back on **left diagonal**, jump on right, left stretched low front, swing arms in <u>frontal plane</u> to right low.

>Counts 3–4: Step left front on left diagonal and jump on left, right leg turned out <u>cou-de-pied</u> behind left, reverse arm movement from counts 1–2.

Measure 50: Step right side on right diagonal, <u>soutenu turn</u> 360 degrees to right, finishing in <u>fifth (V) position</u> <u>relevé</u>, right leg front **facing left diagonal**. During turn, arms down close to body.

Measure 51:

>Counts 1–2: Step right front and jump on right, left leg turned out <u>cou-de-pied</u> behind right. Swing arms in <u>frontal plane</u> to left low.

>Counts 3–4: Step back left, jump on left, right stretched low front, reverse arm movement from counts 1–2.

Measure 52: Slide stretched right leg toward left. Turn 315 degrees to left in <u>relevé</u> to finish **facing audience** in <u>parallel demi-plié</u>, arms close to body.

Measure 53: By stretching both legs, step right side and close left leg to right into <u>parallel demi-plié</u>. Overhead half-circle from left to right in <u>frontal plane</u>, arms following each other, ninety degrees apart, beginning with right, finishing with both arms to right side low.

Measure 54: Small step left to side, and crossing right leg over left, turn 360 degrees to left in relevé to **face audience**. Arms side low during turn.

Measures 55–56: Repeat movement of measures 53–54 to opposite side **facing audience**.

Measure 57:

> Counts 1–2: Step right front and jump on right, left leg in parallel cou-de-pied, arms crossed in front close to body, fingers nearly touching shoulders.

> Counts 3–4: Step back left, jump on left, right stretched low front, open arms front, and continue movement of arms down to close to body.

Measure 58: Two chaines with dorsal side bends toward audience. (See measure 35 for description.) Finish **facing audience**, arms close to body.

Measure 59: Repeat movement of measure 57.

Measure 60: Step right side and repeat movement of measure 58 with chaines parallel with audience. Finish chaines **facing audience**, both arms to right low.

Measure 61: Turn ninety degrees to left with **right shoulder to audience**. Step left forward to lunge and turn 270 degrees to left closing right leg to left, turning in relevé on both feet. Finish **facing audience** in first (I) position relevé. During turn, arms are initially front horizontal and then forearms rotate inward toward body, stretching to horizontal with palms up and finally closing to body.

Measure 62: Repeat movement of measure 61 in opposite direction, but turn only 180 degrees, finishing with **right shoulder to audience**.

Measure 63: Two chaines turns to left (four steps, left, right, left, right), moving straight back away from audience, arms close to body, elbows slightly outward, and fingers touching thighs. Finish standing on left, right leg back on pique with **back to audience**.

Measure 64: Hold legs in position. Raise arms to front horizontal and then rotate forearms inward toward body and stretch arms to V shape in horizontal plane, palms up, and finally close arms to body.

Measures 65 and 66 assume three rows of dancers. Legs remain stationary for all dancers.

Measure 65:

> Counts 1–2:

First row: Raise arms to sides horizontal.

Second and third rows: Keep arms stationary.

Counts 3–4:

Second row: Raise arms to sides horizontal.

First and third rows: Keep arms stationary.

Measure 66:

Counts 1–2:

Third row: Raise arms to sides horizontal.

First and second rows: Keep arms stationary.

Counts 3–4: All dancers lower arms to close to body.

Measure 67: By sliding stretched right leg toward left, turn 180 degrees to right in relevé to **face audience**. Finish in fifth (V) position relevé, right leg front. Raise arms through sides to high overhead into third position of arms.

Measure 68: Turn forty-five degrees to left to **face left diagonal**, and through left cou-de-pied, step left back on left diagonal, right leg front on pique; left arm front horizontal, right arm side horizontal.

Measure 69:

Counts 1–2: Shift weight front to right leg, close arms to body.

Counts 3–4: Turning ninety degrees to right to **face right diagonal**, step left front on right diagonal, arms to left low.

Measure 70: Step right front to lunge. Turn 315 degrees to right on right to **face audience**. Right leg remains in demi-plié during turn; stretched left leg describes arc on floor with toes while turning. Dorsal side bend left during turn, arms to sides in one line, head turned to left. Finish turn in demi-plié on right, left leg side on pique.

Measure 71:

Counts 1–2: Close left leg to right to <u>parallel</u> <u>cou-de-pied</u>, hold in <u>demi-plié</u> on right. Close arms to body with elbows leading, cross forearms in <u>horizontal plane</u> in front of body, palms up.

Counts 3–4: Step left side to <u>second (II) position</u> <u>relevé</u> **facing audience**. Arms open to sides, elbows leading.

Measure 72:

Counts 1–2: Turning forty-five degrees to left to **face left diagonal**, step right to <u>lunge</u>, close arms to body.

Counts 3–4: Turn ninety degrees to right in <u>demi-plié</u> on right to **face right diagonal**. Stretched left leg describes arc on floor with toes. Finish standing on straight right leg facing right diagonal, left leg bent forward, touching floor with ball of foot. During turn swing right arm to side horizontal, left arm remains low behind body. During final pose continue swinging right arm back in <u>horizontal plane</u> and then down in <u>sagittal plane</u>, moving right arm to front. Finally, bend right elbow, fingers of right arm nearly touching left shoulder, <u>dorsal backbend</u>. Look up and point right elbow high.

Muffin Rag

Is everything clear and predictable? Does the

beginning tell you how the ending will be?

Do red skies in the morning always warn of

coming rain?

Muffin Rag

Dancing For Fun
Book 2

Slowly, With Feeling

Mark L. Greathouse

Dance 8: Muffin Rag Choreography

Key Signature: 4/4 changes to 2/4 beginning with measure 27.

Introduction: none

Starting formation: Dancers begin in **staggered rows**.

Starting position: *Left shoulder to audience*, <u>lunge</u> front left, left foot on <u>relevé</u>, weight on left. Right leg, torso, and head are in one line leaning forward, arms crossed behind head in <u>frontal plane</u>, elbows up and fingers touching opposite shoulders.

Measures 1–2: While straightening torso to vertical, step right front, and with weight on right, stretch left <u>leg</u> back <u>on pique.</u> Raise arms starting with elbows, and keeping palms up, lower parallel arms through front to close to body.

Measures 3–4: Cross left leg over right and turn 270 degrees to right in <u>relevé,</u> finishing in <u>first (I) position</u> *facing audience*. Keep arms close to body during turn. At the end of turn, horizontal arc with right arm low from front to side.

Measure 5: Turning forty-five degrees to left, step right over left to *left diagonal*.

Measure 6: Turning ninety degrees to right, step left over right to *right diagonal*.

    Note: During measures 5–6, arms low to sides.

Measures 7–8: Turning forty-five degrees to left to *face audience*, cross right leg over left and turn 450 degrees (one and a quarter circles) to left in <u>relevé</u>, finishing with *right shoulder to audience*, standing on left, right leg <u>parallel</u> bent front, ball of foot touching floor next to left. During turn, arms low to sides and then left arm continues down to close to body, right arm continues down describing arc in <u>sagittal plane</u> to back of body. At end of turn, with impulse and rotating right elbow away from body, bring right arm down in <u>sagittal plane</u> so that both arms are down and limp next to body. Through <u>dorsal front bend</u>, head down, bend body forward to approximately horizontal; continuous arm movement.

Measure 9: Turn ninety degrees to right to **face audience**, and execute four ministeps (step side right, close left to right—repeat four times) to right on <u>relevé</u>. Continue movement of arms and upper body: right arm to describe circle in <u>frontal plane</u>, left arm and upper body follow (right arm down; right arm to left, <u>dorsal side bend</u> to left, left arm side low; right arm up to overhead, straighten body, left arm to side; right arm to right side again and <u>dorsal side bend</u> to right, left arm up). Head follows movement of arms.

Measure 10: Cross left leg over right while lowering left arm to side. Turn 270 degrees to right on <u>relevé</u>. During turn keep both arms in one line while alternating <u>dorsal side bends</u>, first to left, so that right arm is up and left arm is down, and then reverse: Side bend to right, so that left arm is up and right arm is down. Then reverse again: Side bend left with left arm down, right arm up. (During this turn, arms appear to describe circles in <u>frontal plane</u>, from the viewpoint of audience.) Finish in same position as at the end of measure 8 with **right shoulder to audience**.

Measure 11: Repeat movement of measure 9 (ministeps).

Measure 12: Repeat movement of measure 10 (turn with <u>dorsal side bends</u>), but at the end of the turn keep body straight, twist torso to right so that **head faces audience**, arms side low.

Note: Continuous arm movements during measures 5–12.

Measure 13: Turning ninety degrees to right to **face audience**, step right front toward audience on <u>relevé</u>; close left leg to right in <u>fifth (V) position</u> <u>relevé</u>, right leg front. Raise arms to front horizontal, palms up, hands together, one palm in the other. Keeping hands joined and arms from elbow to shoulder stationary, turn forearms (between elbow and wrist) up, then down toward body, and then straighten both joined arms to front and raise to overhead, head up.

Measure 14: Step left back through <u>demi-plié</u> to finish standing on stretched left, right <u>leg</u> front <u>on pique</u>. Keeping hands joined, lower arms to front horizontal, and then keeping arms between elbow and wrist stationary, bend elbows and circle forearms inward and then upward and then downward to horizontal. Release hands, finishing with parallel arms front horizontal, palms up.

Measure 15: Turning forty-five degrees to left, <u>lunge</u> front right on **left diagonal**. Turn ninety degrees to right in <u>demi-plié</u> on right flat foot to finish **facing right diagonal**. During turn, arms to sides, side bend left, and left toes describe arc along floor. Finish in right <u>demi-plié</u>, left <u>leg</u> front <u>on pique</u>.

Measure 16: Through demi-plié, shift weight front onto left and straighten left leg, right leg back on pique facing **right diagonal**. Straighten torso, keep left arm side horizontal. During demi-plié, right arm is front high and with impulse in elbow; turn palm up and lower right arm toward body in sagittal plane.

Measure 17: Through demi-plié, shift weight back onto right and straighten right leg, left leg front on pique. Circle right forearm horizontally inside low front and continue to raise right arm to side horizontal; left arm remains in side horizontal.

Measure 18: Step left back and repeat movement of measure 17 to opposite side, still moving backward **along right diagonal**.

Measure 19: Step right front on relevé and close left leg to right, finishing in fifth (V) position relevé, right leg front. Through sagittal circles front, raise arms to third position of arms.

Measure 20: Through cou-de-pied and demi-plié step left back, right leg front on pique, left arm front horizontal, right arm side horizontal.

Measure 21: Shift weight front onto right, close arms to body.

Measure 22: Step left front into lunge. Prepare left bent arm front low, right arm side low.

Measure 23: Turn 225 degrees to left in demi-plié on left flat foot to finish with **back to audience**. During turn, arms to sides, side bend right and describe arc with right toes along floor. Finish in left demi-plié, right leg front on pique. At end of turn, straighten torso and move arms in frontal plane to left side low.

Measure 24: Step right front into lunge; arms remain stationary.

Measure 25: Repeat turn in demi-plié from measure 23 to opposite side, but with the following change:

> Change: Turn only 180 degrees to finish **facing audience**. Left leg stops moving when reaching side, i.e., finish in side lunge on right, left leg side on pique, arms to sides, side bend left.

Measure 26: Lower arms to body, cross left leg over right, and turn 360 degrees to right on relevé, finishing in fifth (V) position relevé, right leg front.

2/4 music begins:

Measure 27: Step right front and hop on right, left in <u>cou-de-pied</u> behind right. Cross arms in <u>frontal plane</u> close to body, fingers on opposite shoulders.

Measure 28: Step left back and hop on left, right leg stretched front low. Arms remain in position.

Measure 29: Repeat movement of measure 27.

Measure 30: Repeat leg movement of measure 28 with following change:

> Change: Forearms open to front, palms up.

Measure 31: Lower arms to close to body. Step right front and hop on right, turning ninety degrees to right, finishing with **left shoulder to audience**, left leg in <u>cou-de-pied</u> behind right.

Measure 32: Step left back and hop on left, turning 180 degrees to right, finishing with **right shoulder to audience**, right leg in <u>cou-de-pied</u> in front of left. Arms remain close to body.

Measure 33: Step right front and hop on right, turning 180 degrees to right, finishing with **left shoulder to audience**, left leg in <u>cou-de-pied</u> behind right. Arms remain close to body.

Measure 34: Step left back and hop on left, turning 270 degrees to right to finish **facing audience**, right leg in <u>cou-de-pied</u> in front of left. Arms remain close to body.

> Note: In measures 31–34 head is <u>spotting</u> toward audience.

Measures 35–38: Repeat movement of measures 27–30 (series of hops) **facing audience**.

Measures 39–40: Repeat movement of measures 31–32 (continuing series of hops), now executing hops along line parallel with audience, <u>spotting</u> at point ninety degrees right from audience (from point of view of dancer). Finish **facing audience**.

Measure 41: Turning forty-five degrees to right, step right on **right diagonal**. Take off from right; small <u>scissor leap</u> landing in left <u>demi-plié</u>, right <u>leg</u> front <u>on piqué</u>. During leap, left leg is first straight and then bends; right leg is first bent and then straightens. During leap, stretched upper body leans slightly back, forearms execute small circles inward in <u>sagittal plane</u> in front of body. After leap, right arm in front horizontal, left arm side horizontal.

Measure 42: Hold position.

Note: Music now repeats measures 27–42.

Measure 43: Step right on **right diagonal** and hop on right, left in cou-de-pied behind right. Cross arms in frontal plane close to body, fingers on opposite shoulders.

Measure 44: Step left back, hop on left, right leg stretched front low. Arms remain in position.

Measure 45: Step right front turning forty-five degrees to right (**left shoulder to audience**); hop on right, left in cou-de-pied behind right. Arms remain in position.

Measure 46: Step left back, hop on left, right leg stretched front low. Arms remain in position.

Measure 47: Step right front turning ninety degrees to right (**back to audience**); hop on right, left in cou-de-pied behind right. Arms remain in position.

Measures 48: Step left back, hop on left, right leg stretched front low. Open forearms to front horizontal, palms up.

Measures 49–50: Step right side on relevé; soutenu turn 360 degrees to right, finishing with **back to audience**. Arms close to body.

Measure 51: Step right front and hop on right, left in cou-de-pied behind right. Cross arms in frontal plane close to body, fingers on opposite shoulders.

Measure 52: Step left back; hop on left, right leg stretched front low. Arms remain in position.

Measure 53: Step right front turning ninety degrees to right with **right shoulder to audience**; hop on right, left in cou-de-pied behind right. Arms remain in position.

Measure 54: Step left back; hop on left, right leg stretched front low. Arms remain in position.

Measure 55: Step right front turning ninety degrees to right to **face audience**; hop on right, left in cou-de-pied behind right. Arms remain in position.

Measure 56: Step left back; hop on left, right leg stretched front low. Open forearms to front horizontal, palms up.

Measures 57–58: Step right side on relevé; soutenu turn 360 degrees to right, finishing **facing audience**. Arms close to body.

Measures 59-60: Turning forty-five degrees to right, step on **right diagonal** into side <u>lunge</u> on right; lean to right, circle right arm in <u>frontal plane</u> to left, up and to right high, palm up, so that at the end of the measure arms in one line parallel with left leg. Head follows movement of right arm.

Measures 61-62: Shifting weight to left, cross right leg over left. Turn 405 degrees (one and an eighth circles) in <u>relevé</u> to left, arms close to body, finish **facing audience**.

Measure 63: Step right back on <u>relevé</u>, left stretched low front, right arm front horizontal, left arm side horizontal.

Measure 64: Moving back, repeat movement of measure 63 to opposite side.

Measures 65-66: Turning forty-five degrees to left, step right on **left diagonal**. Taking off from right, small <u>scissor leap</u>, landing in left <u>demi-plié</u>, right <u>leg</u> front <u>on piqué</u>. During leap, left leg is first straight and then bends; right leg is first bent and then straightens. During leap, stretched upper body leans slightly back; forearms execute small circles inward in <u>sagittal plane</u> in front of body. After leap, left arm in front horizontal, right arm side horizontal.

Measures 67-68: Stepping right front on <u>relevé</u>, turn 270 degrees to left in <u>relevé</u> while closing stretched left leg to right. Finish **facing right diagonal** in <u>fifth (V) position</u> <u>relevé</u>, left leg front, arms close to body.

Measures 69-70: Step left on **right diagonal** and repeat movement of measures 65-66 to opposite side (small <u>scissor leap</u>).

Measures 71-72: Closing left leg to right to <u>fifth (V) position</u> <u>relevé</u>, left leg front, turn 225 degrees to right on <u>relevé</u>, finishing with **right shoulder to audience** in <u>fifth (V) position</u> <u>relevé</u>, right leg front, arms close to body.

Measures 73-74: Turning ninety degrees to right to **face audience**, step right front toward audience and turn 360 degrees to right on stretched right leg with slight <u>relevé</u>, left leg <u>parallel</u> bent at knee, close to right, left ball of foot brushing floor. Finish **facing audience**. Arms closed to body.

Note: Measures 75-77 assume three rows of dancers. Movement is done in <u>canon</u>.

Measure 75:

First row: Turn ninety degrees to left, shifting weight to left leg. Finish with **_right shoulder to audience_** standing on left, right leg <u>parallel</u> bent at knee, close to left, right ball of foot touching floor. Upper body turned to right to face audience. Cross arms in <u>frontal plane</u> close to body, fingers on opposite shoulders. Head down.

Second and third rows: Hold previous position.

Measure 76:

Second row: Repeat movement of first row from measure 75.

All other rows hold positions.

Measure 77:

Third row: Repeat movement of first row from measure 75.

All other rows hold positions.

Measure 78: All dancers lower slightly front bend of body.

Measure 79: Turn forty-five degrees to right to **_face right diagonal_**, step on right heel, right leg stretched. Arms follow each other gradually, head follows movement of arms, torso straight. Starting with right arm, straighten right arm to left low and then move it in <u>frontal plane</u> to left, then up while straightening left arm to left side low. Keeping angle of about ninety degrees between arms, start to move them gradually overhead in <u>frontal plane</u> to right.

Measure 80: Turn forty-five degrees to right to **_face audience_**. Step on left heel, left leg stretched into <u>second (II) position</u> on heels. Continue movement of arms in <u>frontal plane</u> to right.

Measure 81: Step right side and turn ninety degrees to right, **_left shoulder to audience_**. Continue arm movement in same direction from previous measure, right arm finishing movement with close to body.

Measure 82: Cross left leg over right. Left arm finishes movement so that at end of measure both arms close to body.

Measure 83: Turn 180 degrees to right to finish with **right shoulder to audience**, standing on stretched left, right <u>parallel</u> bent front, ball of right foot touching floor.

Note: In measure 84 continuous movement of arms and legs.

Measure 84: Through sliding right leg back along floor, <u>lunge</u> on left, right arm inward circle and stretch back parallel with right leg, left hand on left hip. Turn 180 degrees to right, finishing with **left shoulder to audience**, and shift weight to right leg to end in <u>lunge</u> on right, right arm front horizontal. Through sliding left toes along floor, close left leg to right and lower right arm to close to body. Finish standing on stretched right leg, left <u>parallel</u> bent front, ball of left foot touching floor.

Measures 85-114: Turn ninety degrees to left *to* **face audience** and repeat movement of measures 27-56 (hops and small <u>scissor leap</u>).

Measure 115: Repeat movement of measures 65-66 (small <u>scissor leap</u>). Here we have movement of two measures now executed in this **one measure**.

Measure 116: Step right front and turn 180 degrees to left, finishing on **left back diagonal** (facing away from audience). <u>Lunge</u> front left, left foot in <u>relevé</u>, weight on left. Right leg, torso and head are in one line leaning forward, arms crossed behind head in <u>frontal plane</u>, elbows up and fingers touching opposite shoulders. This final configuration is same as starting position.

Snowfall

The pristine, white snow falling can be
beautiful to watch. But sometimes
the wind rises and a blizzard is born.

Snowfall

Dancing For Fun
Book 2

With Feeling

Mark L. Greathouse

Dance 9: Snowfall Choreography

Key Signature: 2/4

Introduction: 8 measures

Starting formation: Dancers in **V shape**, point closest to audience.

Starting position: With *back to audience*, stand on right, bent left leg crossed behind right, touching floor with ball of foot, arms close to body, head down.

Measure 1: Step left front away from audience, head up.

Measure 2: Demi-plié on left, raise arms slightly to sides, close right leg to left so that right leg has same position as left leg had in starting position.

Measure 3: Hold legs in demi-plié; lower arms to close to body.

Measure 4: Relevé in fifth (V) position, left leg front, raise arms through sides to third position of arms, look up.

Measure 5: Step right front away from audience; open arms to sides, palms up, look up and chest up.

Measure 6: Close left leg to right into parallel demi-plié, legs together. Continue movement of arms: left to side low, right to close to body.

Measures 7–8: Turn 180 degrees to right through relevé to parallel demi-plié, legs together, to *face audience*. Right arm continues circle in frontal plane to left, up, to right and down; keep left arm side low and head follows movement of right arm.

Measures 9–10: Continue right arm movement in frontal plane down to left and then windmill arms right. When arms are up, relevé on both legs; when arms are to right, finish in parallel demi-plié, legs together.

Measure 11: Straighten left leg and immediately relevé on left, small parallel develope with right leg forward, open arms to sides.

Measure 12: Step into right demi-plié front, close left leg to right so that left leg is as in starting position. With chest first leading, follow with dorsal front bend. With elbows leading, lower arms so that they are parallel and vertical in front of body.

Measures 13-14: Parallel demi-plié, legs together. Repeat movement of measures 9-10 (windmill arms and parallel develope).

Measure 15: Repeat movement of measure 11 (parallel develope) to opposite side, still facing audience, but increase amplitude of develope (perhaps to forty-five degrees).

Measure 16: Repeat movement of measure 12 (dorsal front bend) to opposite side.

Measures 17-18: Turning ninety degrees to right with **left shoulder to audience**, parallel demi-plié, legs together. Repeat movement of measures 9-10 (windmill arms and parallel develope).

Measure 19: Repeat movement of measure 11 (parallel develope) to opposite side, but still more increase of amplitude of develope (perhaps to ninety degrees).

Measure 20: Repeat movement of measure 12 (dorsal front bend) to opposite side.

Measures 21-22: Turning ninety degrees to right with **back to audience**, step right side on relevé in second (II) position and repeat arm movement of measures 9-10 (windmill arms), finishing in demi-plié on right, close left leg to right, weight on right, left leg parallel bent and on ball of foot, knees together.

Measures 23-24: Reverse movement of measures 21-22 omitting the initial turn. At the end, turn ninety degrees to left with **left shoulder to audience**, head to left, keeping both feet in same place on the floor as they were in second (II) position. Finish on left in demi-plié, right leg crossed behind left, legs not touching, both arms left low, torso straight.

Measures 25-26: Turning ninety degrees to left to **face audience**, step right into side lunge, move arms in frontal plane through down to right side, so that right arm is higher than left arm; lean to right, head right.

Measures 27-28: Shift weight to left, cross right leg over left, turn 450 degrees (one and a quarter circles) to left in relevé to finish with **right shoulder to audience**. Close arms to body.

Measures 29-32: Chaines to right, arms close to body, to dissolve the initial V shape and finish in **one column** in the center of the dance space **facing audience**. (Dancer number one, who is at the point where the lines meet in a "V," travels toward the audience during the <u>chaines</u>. Remaining dancers vary the length of steps in <u>chaines</u> so that they form a single column behind the first dancer.)

Note: In measures 33–40 dancers remain in place in single column.

Measure 33:

Odd-numbered dancers execute right <u>arm wave</u> side.

Even-numbered dancers execute left <u>arm wave</u> side.

Measure 34: Reverse movement of measure 33.

Measures 35–36: Repeat movement of measures 33–34.

Measures 37–38: Through <u>parallel demi-plié,</u> straighten both legs and rise to <u>relevé</u>. Raise arms sideways and continue them up to <u>third position of arms</u>, head up.

Measures 39–40: Through lowering heels and subsequent <u>parallel demi-plié</u>, straighten knees to stand in <u>first (I) position</u>. Lower arms sideways to close to body. Dancers ***face audience***.

Note: **Even-numbered dancers** execute movement of measures 41–64 to opposite side, in **mirror image** to odd-numbered dancers. Therefore only the movement of odd-numbered dancers is described below.

Note: **Odd-numbered dancers** measures 41–64:

Measures 41–42: Turning ninety degrees to left with ***right shoulder to audience***, left <u>lunge</u> forward, left arm front horizontal, right arm behind body horizontal and <u>chaines</u> to left, parallel with audience, arms close to body. Finish <u>chaines</u> with ***right shoulder to audience***.

Measure 43: Step right front on <u>relevé</u>, left leg <u>parallel develope</u> to forty-five degrees front, arms circle front, up and back in <u>sagittal plane;</u> head and chest up when arms are up.

Measure 44: Step front on straight left leg, close turned-out bent right leg to left, right leg touching floor with ball of foot behind left leg, arms close to body.

Measures 45–46: Turning ninety degrees to right to ***face audience***, step right front on <u>relevé</u> and <u>soutenu turn</u> 270 degrees to right, finishing in <u>fifth (V) position</u> <u>relevé</u> right leg front, with ***right shoulder to audience***. Arms close to body.

Measure 47: Turning forty-five degrees to right to **face left diagonal**, repeat movement of measure 43 (parallel develope).

Measure 48: Repeat movement of measure 44, facing left diagonal.

Measures 49-52: Four walking steps (right, left, right, left) along arc to right, turning 135 degrees to right, finishing with **left shoulder to audience**, arms port de bras, low front to open to low sides, close to body on last step. Finish standing on left, right leg back on pique, arms back low.

> Note: Now dancers are in couples facing each other in **two columns**.

> Note: Measures 53-54 are performed in canon (assuming **four** groups of dancers). Each group performs the following movement on its **assigned count**. Therefore each group must react quickly.

Measures 53-54:

> Reminder: The following description takes place in one count. This movement will occur four times within these two measures.

Through dorsal bend arching with chest leading, move upper body down to vertical, ending with head down and finishing in dorsal front bend, arms parallel and vertical. Simultaneously demi-plié on left; close right leg to left by sliding along floor, finishing with right behind left on ball of foot, right knee bent and turned out.

> Note: From measure 55 on, all dancers perform simultaneously.

Measures 55-56: Slowly and gradually straighten body, one vertebra at a time, and straighten left support leg.

Measure 57: Step right front.

Measure 58: Turning ninety degrees to right with **back to audience**, step left front away from audience.

Measures 59-60: Turning ninety degrees to right with **right shoulder to audience**, step right front on relevé and turn 180 degrees to right in low arabesque, finishing with **left shoulder to audience**, legs together in parallel demi-plié, and subsequently straighten legs. During arabesque turn, right arm front high, head follows movement of right arm, left arm low back. During demi-plié, close arms to body.

Measures 61-64: Repeat movement of measures 57-60 (steps and arabesque turn) to opposite side, but with change.

Change: Arabesque turn is 270 degrees to finish **facing audience**.

Note: Until now dancers were moving while maintaining two columns.

Note: During measures 65-68, dancers dissolve two columns and move into **staggered lines parallel with audience**. All dancers now perform the **same movement**. However, each dancer takes steps of various lengths and in various directions in order to arrive at correct location.

Measures 65-68: Take two steps (right, left), followed by arabesque turn (described in measures 59-60) on right to right, finishing **facing audience** (dancers now in staggered lines).

Measure 69:

Count 1: Parallel demi-plié on left, lift bent right leg low front, right toes at left ankle, cross arms in front of body, elbows nearly touching body, forearms horizontal, palms up.

Count 2: Step right side into second (II) position relevé; open arms to sides.

Measure 70: Shifting weight to left and crossing right leg over left, step right to lunge on right to **face left diagonal**. Prepare both arms to left low.

Measures 71-72: Turn 405 degrees (one and an eighth circles) to right on right, left leg low in arabesque, torso straight, right arm front high, left arm back low. Finish **facing audience** in parallel demi-plié, legs together, arms close to body.

Measures 73-103: Repeat movement of measures 9-40. Finish **facing audience**.

Measure 104:

Odd-numbered dancers cross right over left and turn ninety degrees to left with **right shoulder to audience**.

Even-numbered dancers stand without movement.

Measure 105:

Odd-numbered dancers stand without movement.

Even-numbered dancers cross left over right and turn ninety degrees to right with *left shoulder to audience*.

Note: Odd- and even-numbered dancers are now in **two columns with backs to each other**.

Note: **Even-numbered dancers** execute movement of measures 106–110 to opposite side, in **mirror image** to odd-numbered dancers. Therefore only the movement of odd-numbered dancers is described below.

Note: **Odd-numbered dancers** in measures 106–110:

Measure 106: Step left front. Close right leg to left so that right heel is at left ankle, ball of foot touching floor, right leg parallel bent front. Turn head to right to **face audience**.

Measure 107: Two jumps from both to both to right side, dorsal side bend left, both arms to right in frontal plane, look at right arm (moving toward audience).

Measure 108: Reverse direction and repeat movement of measure 107 to left (away from audience).

Note: **Even-numbered dancers** also move in measures 107–108, first toward and then away from audience.

Measures 109–110: Cross left leg over right. Turn 450 degrees (one and a quarter circles) to right to *face audience*, arms close to body.

Note: In measures 111–112 dancers **dissolve both columns** and return to **staggered lines**. Therefore dancers move in various directions. Movement is same for all dancers. All dancers finish *facing audience*.

Measures 111–112: Repeat movement of measures 107–108 (jumps from both to both) as written, now moving parallel with audience, first to right and then to left.

Measures 113–114: Cross right leg over left and turn 270 degrees to left to finish with *left shoulder to audience*, arms close to body.

Measure 115:

> Count 1: Step right front to <u>lunge</u>, stretch left arm front horizontal, right arm low back.

> Count 2: Through small <u>parallel</u> <u>develope</u> front, move left <u>leg</u> front <u>on pique</u>. Swing right arm front, bent elbow, and put palm close to head as if touching ear, left arm back, wrist flexed upward. Turn body left toward audience.

Measure 116:

> Count 1: Step left back, right arm low back, left arm low front.

> Count 2: <u>Demi-plié</u> on left, and through small <u>parallel</u> <u>develope</u> back, move right leg to back, ball of foot touching floor. Swing right arm to low front, left arm back, both wrists slightly flexed upward. Turn body left toward audience.

Measures 117–118: Starting with right, four <u>Charleston steps</u> forward, arms moving in <u>sagittal plane</u> from low back to low front and reverse. If Charleston is on right, left arm is forward and vice versa. Finish standing on left, right leg bent, ball of foot touching floor back away from left leg, arms low sides.

Measures 119–120: Repeat movement of measures 115–116.

Measure 121: Starting with right, two <u>Charleston steps</u> forward, arms moving in <u>sagittal plane</u> from low back to low front and reverse. If Charleston is on right, left arm is forward and vice versa. Finish standing on left, right leg bent, ball of foot touching floor back away from left leg, arms low sides.

Measure 122:

> Count 1: Taking off from both feet, small vertical jump, landing in <u>second (II) position</u> <u>demi-plié</u>. Quick movement of arms, elbows leading, first to front, elbows together, forearms with palms facing up. Turning elbows outward, stretch arms quickly to V shape up.

> Count 2: Taking off from both feet, small vertical jump turning ninety degrees left to *face audience*, landing in <u>parallel</u> <u>first (I) position</u> demi-plié. Close arms through sides to body.

Measures 123–124: Repeat movement of measures 115–116 with change.

Change: In count 2 of measure 123, right arm front horizontal.

Measures 125–126: Repeat movement of measures 123–124.

Measures 127–128: Turning ninety degrees to right with **left shoulder to audience**, repeat movement of measures 115–116 as written.

Measure 129: Repeat movement of measure 115 as written.

Measures 130: Close arms to body, cross left leg over right, and turn in <u>relevé</u> 270 degrees to right, finishing in <u>first (I) position</u> **facing audience**.

Note: In measures 131–134 legs are always slightly bent at knees.

Measure 131: Pushing right hip to side, step right side and circle right shoulder forward; turn head to right and then close left leg to right.

Measure 132: Repeat movement of measure 131 to opposite side.

Measure 133: Repeat movement of measure 131 with change.

Change: Turn torso forty-five degrees to right and move **along right diagonal forward**.

Measure 134: Repeat movement of measure 133.

Measure 135: Repeat leg movements of measure 131 to opposite side, starting with left. Swing arms first to left in <u>frontal plane</u> so that left arm finishes slightly above horizontal, <u>dorsal side bend</u> to right, turn head to left.

Measure 136: Same as movement of measure 135 but to opposite side.

Measures 137–138: Cross right over left and turn 360 degrees to left to **face audience**, arms close to body.

Measures 139–140: Repeat movement of measures 111–112 (<u>jumps from both to both</u>, moving parallel with audience).

Measures 141–142: Cross right leg over left, arms close to body. Turn 270 degrees to left in <u>relevé</u>, finishing with **left shoulder to audience**.

Measures 143-144: Repeat movement of measures 111-112 (jumps from both to both, moving parallel with audience).

Measures 145-146: Cross right leg over left, arms close to body. Turn 450 degrees (one and a quarter circles) to left in relevé to finish **facing audience**.

Measures 147-148: Repeat movement of measures 115-116 with change.

Change: In count 2 of measure 147, right arm front horizontal.

Measures 149-150: Repeat movement of measures 117-118 (four Charleston steps).

Measures 151-152: Repeat movement of measures 147-148.

Measure 153: Repeat movement of measure 122 (vertical jumps) with change.

Change: In count 2 turn 180 degrees to left, landing on left leg with **right shoulder to audience**, right leg bent ninety degrees with right knee touching left knee, arms low side.

Measure 154:

Count 1: Step right front, cross arms low in front of body, palms down.

Count 2: Move stretched left leg in sagittal plane forward and touch floor with ball of left foot, left knee bent with lower leg vertical. Turning palms up and bending elbows, move arms in sagittal plane back as far as possible and look up.

Medieval Waltz

God plants a seed in our heart.

When we nourish it, it blossoms.

Medieval Waltz

Dancing For Fun
Book 2

Mark L. Greathouse

Medieval Waltz ♫ 127

Dance 10: Medieval Waltz Parts 1-5 Choreography

This dance uses one scarf per dancer in parts one and five of the dance. Ideally the scarf should be square and made of light material, each side approximately two or three feet long. The scarf will always be held on upper corners, stretched (not limp), and hanging down, unless otherwise noted. The upper side of the scarf being held will be horizontal.

One dancer is designated as a soloist. This dancer is in the center, three steps in front of the first row.

Key Signature: 3/4

Introduction: 3 notes prior to start of dance

Part 1

Starting formation: Dancers begin in **staggered lines** (number of lines depends on the number of dancers).

Starting position: Facing right diagonal, stand on left, bent turned-out right leg crossed behind left, right pointed toes touching floor about one foot away from left heel. Arms down on left side of body, holding scarf on upper corners, scarf hanging down in <u>sagittal plane</u>, head down.

> Note: Head follows movement of scarf in measures 1–3.

Measure 1:

> Counts 1–2: Through <u>demi-plié</u> on left, step back on right <u>relevé</u>, lift stretched left leg low (forty-five degrees) front. Move stretched arms to front horizontal; scarf hangs down in <u>frontal plane</u>.

> Count 3: Step left front to <u>demi-plié</u>, right leg <u>cou-de-pied</u> behind left; lower scarf down in <u>frontal plane</u>.

Measure 2:

       Counts 1–2: Repeat movement of counts 1–2 from measure 1 with change.

       Change: Lift left leg to horizontal; lift scarf to front high.

       Count 3: Same as count 3 measure 1.

Measure 3: Turning ninety degrees to right, torso facing **left back diagonal**, side <u>lunge</u> right along right diagonal, head to right, <u>arms in frontal plane</u> to right.

Measure 4: Shift weight to left, cross right leg over left, and turn 135 degrees to left in <u>relevé</u> to **face audience** in <u>fifth (V) position</u> <u>relevé</u>, right leg front. During turn perform <u>figure eight</u>, right arm leading. At end, scarf hangs behind body in <u>frontal plane</u>.

Measure 5: Step left side and <u>balance step</u> left. With side bend to right, move arms in <u>horizontal plane</u> in front of body to left, finishing with <u>arms in frontal plane</u> to left.

Measure 6: Step right side and <u>balance step</u> right. Move arms first to front high and then lower arms to finish with <u>arms in frontal plane</u> to right.

Measure 7: Turn ninety degrees to left with **right shoulder to audience**; through <u>demi-plié</u> on left, straighten left leg, right <u>leg</u> back <u>on pique</u>. With impulse in right arm, describe arc to left in <u>horizontal plane</u> so that scarf flies horizontally. Finish with right arm crossed over left, bend elbows and raise them toward ceiling, <u>dorsal backbend</u>, look up; scarf hangs in <u>frontal plane</u> in front of body.

Measure 8: Hold in position.

Measure 9: <u>Arabesque scale</u> on left, head up and turned right toward audience. Right arm describes arc to right in <u>horizontal plane</u> back so that at end of measure, scarf is hanging in <u>sagittal plane</u> on right side of body, upper edge of scarf horizontal.

Measure 10: Straighten torso, right <u>leg</u> back <u>on pique</u>. Repeat arm and torso movement from measure 7.

Measure 11: Through <u>parallel</u> <u>develope</u> of right leg front and through <u>demi-plié</u> on left, <u>relevé</u> on left, right leg stretched front horizontal. Continue movement of arms to perform <u>figure eight</u>, right arm leading. Finish with both arms up; scarf hangs in <u>frontal plane</u> behind body.

Measure 12: Step right front to stand on right, <u>parallel</u> left bent front, ball of left foot touching floor next to right foot. With <u>dorsal side bend</u> to right, both arms move to right side, keeping scarf stretched. Straighten torso, move arms from right to front, keeping left arm above and parallel with right arm, scarf stretched; continue arm movement diagonally to left low, finishing left arm behind body, right arm slightly in front of body on left side. Scarf hangs down in sagittal plane on left side of body.

Measure 13: Cross left leg over right, turn 495 degrees (one and a quarter circles plus forty-five degrees) in relevé to right to **face right diagonal**, finishing in parallel demi-plié on both legs. During turn, perform figure eight, left arm leading. Continue to move both arms front and then to right low, finishing with right arm behind body, left arm slightly in front of body on right side. Scarf hangs down in sagittal plane right.

Measure 14: Hold legs in position. Move arms with scarf farther back in sagittal plane; turn head to left to look at audience.

Measure 15:

> Count 1: Step left to demi-plié along right diagonal. Through circle in sagittal plane back and up with right arm, cross right arm over left in front of body; keep torso straight, look toward audience.

> Counts 2-3: Relevé on left, and through parallel develope, stretch right leg front to horizontal (or higher). Through circle in sagittal plane front down and up on left side of body with right arm, left arm follows right arm; keep torso straight, look forward on right diagonal, head follows movement of arms.

Measure 16:

> Count 1: Step right front to stand on right, parallel left bent front, ball of left foot touching floor next to right foot. Both arms move in sagittal plane front and down, both finishing left low, left arm behind body, right arm slightly in front of body on left side. Scarf hangs down in sagittal plane left.

> Counts 2-3: Cross left leg over right and turn 315 degrees to right in relevé, finishing in fifth (V) position relevé, right leg front, **facing audience**. Arms remain in position; scarf flies behind dancers during rotation.

Measure 17: Step left side and balance step left. Raise arms in horizontal plane in front of body and then to right, finishing with arms in frontal plane to right.

Measure 18: Step right side and <u>balance step</u> right while performing <u>figure eight</u>, right arm leading. Finish with both arms up; scarf hangs in <u>frontal plane</u> behind body.

Measures 19–20: Repeat movement of measures 17–18.

Measure 21: Turning forty-five degrees to right to **face right diagonal**, repeat movement of measure 17.

Measure 22: Turning forty-five degrees to right with **left shoulder to audience**, step right front on <u>relevé</u> and close stretched left leg to right into <u>fifth (V) position</u> <u>relevé</u>, right leg front. Perform <u>figure eight</u>, right arm leading. Finish with both arms up; scarf hangs in <u>frontal plane</u> behind body and look up.

Measure 23: Step right front on <u>relevé</u>, left leg bent in <u>parallel passé</u>. Keeping arms straight and parallel to each other, move them front down and then to left, finishing with arms low on left side of body, right slightly front, left back. Scarf hangs in <u>sagittal plane</u> left. Turn head left toward audience.

Measure 24: Cross left over right and turn 225 degrees to right in <u>relevé</u> to **face left diagonal**, finishing in <u>fifth (V) position</u> <u>relevé</u>, right leg front. Perform <u>circle arms</u> left, finishing with both arms up; scarf hangs in <u>frontal plane</u> behind body.

Measure 25:

> Counts 1–2: Step right front on <u>relevé</u> and raise left leg to low <u>arabesque</u> (forty-five degrees). Keeping arms straight and parallel to each other, move them front down and then to right, finishing with <u>arms in frontal plane</u> to right.

> Count 3: Step left front to slight <u>demi-plié</u>. Keep <u>arms in frontal plane</u> to right; scarf flies during step along left diagonal.

Measure 26: Step right front on <u>relevé</u> and turn 360 degrees on right to left, left leg in <u>cou-de-pied</u> in front. Keep left arm stationary and describe low horizontal circle front with right arm, so that at end of turn, right arm is crossed over left. Both arms low front and slightly bent; scarf hangs down in <u>frontal plane</u>.

Measure 27:

> Counts 1–2: Step left front and then step right front on <u>relevé</u> and raise left leg to low <u>arabesque</u> (forty-five degrees). Keep arms straight and parallel to

each other while raising them front and up. Scarf flies and finishes hanging in <u>frontal plane</u> behind body. Look up.

Count 3: Step left front to slight <u>demi-plié</u>, right <u>leg</u> front <u>on pique</u>. Keep arms straight and parallel to each other while moving them front down. Finish with <u>arms in frontal plane</u> to left.

Measure 28: Turning forty-five degrees to right to **face audience**, step right front on <u>relevé</u> and turn 360 degrees <u>soutenu turn</u> to right. During turn, first put left hand to right hip and describe horizontal circle with right arm to left (opposite direction of turn). Move left arm to left high and continue circle of right arm to right high behind body. Dancer actually turns under the scarf. Finish in <u>fifth (V) position</u> <u>relevé</u>, left leg front, facing audience, both arms up; scarf hangs in <u>frontal plane</u> behind body. Look up.

Measure 29: By crossing left leg over right, turn forty-five degrees to right and <u>lunge</u> on left, **facing right diagonal**, right heel touching floor. Side bend to left, arms describe horizontal arc to right, right arm above left. Finish with arms low on right side of body, left slightly front, right back; scarf hangs in <u>sagittal plane</u> right. Turn head left toward audience.

Measure 30: With impulse from right leg, turn ninety degrees to left on left flat foot; right toes describe circle on floor. During turn, right arm follows right leg, left hand holds scarf close to body and does not move. Finish in <u>fifth (V) position</u> <u>relevé</u>, right leg front, **facing left diagonal**. Continue circle of right arm to left high and behind body to right high. Finish with arms up; scarf hangs behind body in <u>frontal plane</u>.

Measure 31: Through small <u>parallel</u> <u>develope</u>, step left front, right <u>leg</u> back <u>on pique</u>. Keeping arms straight and parallel to each other, move them forward to front horizontal and then down. Scarf hangs in <u>frontal plane</u> in front of body, head down.

Measure 32: Hold position.

Measures 33–35: Repeat movement of measures 1–3, traveling backward along left diagonal.

Change: In measure 35 the turn is forty-five degrees to **face audience**.

Measure 36: Step side left on <u>relevé</u> and <u>soutenu turn</u> 360 degrees to left to face audience. Repeat arm movement from measure 4 (<u>figure eight</u>).

Measures 37–38: Repeat movement of measures 5–6 (<u>balance steps</u>).

Measure 39: Turn forty-five degrees to left to **face left diagonal**; step left front, right leg back on pique. With impulse in right arm, describe arc to left in horizontal plane so that scarf flies horizontally. Finish with right arm crossed over left at waist level close to body. Scarf hangs in frontal plane in front of body.

Measure 40: Hold in position.

Measure 41: Repeat movement of measure 9 (arabesque scale).

Measure 42: Bend turned-out right leg and turn ninety degrees to right on stretched left leg, flat foot, to **face right diagonal**, and stretch right leg front to horizontal. Keep torso low in dorsal backbend. Circle arms right. Finish with arms up; scarf hangs behind body in frontal plane.

> Note: The soloist should be able to perform movements of measures 41–42 in full amplitude. Others may perform with less amplitude, but they should perform in a uniform way.

Measure 43: Through relevé on left, step right front. Keep arms straight and parallel to each other, moving them forward to front horizontal and then down to left. Scarf hangs in sagittal plane on left side of body. Close left leg to right by sliding toes on floor, finishing standing on right, left bent parallel front, left toes touching floor next to right foot. Turn head left to look at audience.

Measure 44: Cross left leg over right and turn 315 degrees to right in relevé to **face audience** in fifth (V) position relevé, right leg front. During turn, circle arms left and follow with movement through front to low right.

Measure 45: Side lunge right, head to right, arms in frontal plane to right.

Measure 46: Shift weight to left, cross right leg over left, turn 315 degrees in relevé to left to **face right diagonal** in parallel demi-plié. Circle arms right until both arms up; scarf hangs in frontal plane behind body. Change direction by swinging right arm front down in sagittal plane, and continue up behind body, finishing low back, left arm front low on right side of body. At the end, scarf hangs in sagittal plane on right side of body.

Measures 47–48: Repeat movement of measures 15–16 (parallel develope and circles in sagittal plane). Finish **facing audience**.

> Note: Between measures 49 and 55 distance between lines of dancers decreases.

Measure 49: Step left side and <u>balance step</u> left. Raise arms in <u>horizontal plane</u> in front of body. Lower them to left, finishing with <u>arms in frontal plane</u> to left.

Measure 50: Step right side and <u>balance step</u> right. Perform <u>figure eight</u> right. After reaching position when arms are up and scarf behind body in <u>frontal plane</u>, continue arm movement, lowering arms sideways to right.

Measure 51: Step left side on <u>relevé</u>, <u>soutenu turn</u> 360 degrees to left, finish **facing audience** in <u>fifth (V) position</u> <u>relevé</u>, left leg front. Repeat arm movement from measure 50; continue arm movement to front and left side, finishing with scarf in <u>frontal plane</u>, arms to left.

Measure 52: Hold in position.

Measures 53–55: Repeat movement of measures 49–51 to opposite side with change.

> Change: Replace <u>figure eight</u> in measure 54 with arm movement from measure 49.

Measure 56: Repeat movement of measure 29 to <u>lunge</u> on left, **facing right diagonal**.

Measure 57: With impulse from right leg, turn forty-five degrees to left on left flat foot to **face audience**; right toes describe circle on floor. During turn, right arm follows right leg, left hand holds scarf close to body and does not move. Cross right leg over left, turn 360 degrees to left, and continue with both arms to left, behind body and to right, and again front and to left side horizontal. Finish **facing audience** in <u>fifth (V) position</u> <u>relevé</u>, left leg front. Scarf hangs down in <u>frontal plane</u> on left side of body.

Measure 58: Step side right to <u>lunge</u> on right, arms to side right, head to right.

Measure 59: Shift weight to left, cross right leg over left, turn 315 degrees to left to **face right diagonal**; finish in <u>fifth (V) position</u> <u>relevé</u>, left leg front. During turn cross right hand over left at waist level. Finish with scarf in front of body, hanging in <u>frontal plane</u>.

> Note: Between measures 61 and 63 back lines of dancers move forward so that at the end of measure 62 all dancers are in one line and scarves are dropped at the edge of the stage.

Measure 61: Moving along **right diagonal**, repeat movement of measure 25 (first <u>arabesque</u>).

Measure 62: Step right front on <u>relevé</u> and turn 360 degrees on right to right, left leg <u>cou-de-pied</u> back. Arms low.

Measure 63: Step left front on <u>relevé</u>, right in low <u>arabesque</u> (forty-five degrees). Raise arms front and high. At highest point release scarf front.

Measure 64: Step right front, left <u>leg</u> back <u>on pique</u>, arms close to body, head down.

Part 2

Starting formation: Dancers are in **one row** with soloist in the middle. This row is as far forward toward audience as possible.

Starting position: Facing *right diagonal*, stand on right, left <u>leg</u> back <u>on pique</u>, arms close to body, head down.

> Note: Dancers divide into two groups: odd- and even-numbered dancers. Soloist is now in same row with other dancers (in the middle) and must be odd numbered. The two dancers next to the soloist must be even numbered, next pair odd numbered, etc. Counting is from the middle.

Description of **even-numbered dancers' movement** in measures 65–68 (**as shown on video**):

> Note: Even-numbered dancers move as far back on stage as possible and are in one row at the back of the stage.

Measure 65: Cross left leg over right, turn 405 degrees (one circle plus forty-five degrees) to right to finish with *left shoulder to audience*, arms close to body.

Measure 66: Two <u>chaines</u> turns to right (right, left, right, left) away from audience, arms close to body.

Measures 67–68: Turning forty-five degrees to right, step on *right back diagonal*, right arm front horizontal, left arm side horizontal. Turn 180 degrees to right on right, left leg in <u>cou-de-pied</u> behind right, <u>first position of arms</u>. With force put left foot to floor behind right foot, and execute small turning <u>jeté</u> leap (turn 180 degrees to right), right leg front, both legs stretched, taking off from left. During <u>jeté</u> leap, slight <u>dorsal backbend</u> and swing right arm to front horizontal, left arm to back horizontal. Look over right shoulder. Land on right and immediately step left front on *right back diagonal*, right <u>leg</u> back <u>on pique</u>. Arms close to body.

Description of **odd-numbered dancers' movement** in measures 65–68:

> Measures 65–66: Hold legs in position, raise arms slowly to side horizontal.

Measures 67–68: Hold legs in position, lower arms slowly to close to body.

Description of **odd-numbered dancers' movement** in measures 69–72:

> Same (with change below) as even-numbered dancers in measures 65–68, but dancers don't move back as far as the row of even-numbered dancers. There are then two parallel rows: odd-numbered dancers' row is in front of even-numbered dancers' row. Odd-numbered dancers stand in staggered formation so that they don't stand directly in front of even-numbered dancers.

> Change: Immediately after landing on right and stepping left front on **right back diagonal**, quickly turn 180 degrees to right in left demi-plié to **face right diagonal**, right leg front on pique. Bend elbows in horizontal and place hands on opposite shoulders. Straighten left leg and raise elbows up, dorsal backbend. Look up.

Description of **even-numbered dancers' movement** in measures 69–72 (**as shown on video**):

Measure 69: Hold legs in position, raise arms slowly to side horizontal.

Measure 70: Hold legs in position, lower arms slowly to close to body.

Measure 71: Demi-plié on left. Keep right leg back on pique (right leg slides backward). Raise straight arms to front horizontal, crossing right arm over left.

Measure 72: Turn 180 degrees to right in left demi-plié to **face right diagonal**, right leg front on pique. Bend elbows in horizontal and place hands on opposite shoulders. Straighten left leg and raise elbows up, dorsal backbend. Look up.

> Note: From now on all dancers perform the same movement simultaneously.

Measure 73:

> Counts 1–2: Step right front on relevé **along right diagonal**, left leg in low arabesque (forty-five degrees). Keeping elbows stationary, open forearms front to horizontal, palms up.

> Count 3: Step left front, lower arms to body, elbows leading, palms up.

Measure 74:

> Counts 1–2: Step right front on <u>relevé</u> along right diagonal, left leg in <u>cou-de-pied</u> behind right leg, and turn 360 degrees on right to right, arms close to body.

> Count 3: Step left front into <u>demi-plié</u>, right <u>leg</u> back <u>on pique</u>. Hold arms close to body.

Measure 75:

> Counts 1–2: Turning forty-five degrees to left to **face audience**, <u>develope</u> with right leg to side through turned out <u>passé</u>, side bend to right, open arms to sides. Continue with left arm in <u>frontal plane</u> overhead so that fingers are pointed to right side.

> Count 3: Straighten standing left leg. Hold position of body and arms.

Measure 76: Straighten body, cross right leg over left, and turn 450 degrees (one and a quarter circles) to left in <u>relevé</u> on both legs, finishing in <u>first (I) position</u> <u>relevé</u> with **right shoulder to audience**. Arms close to body.

Measure 77: Step left front and <u>arabesque scale</u> on left. Straighten arms to front so that right leg, arms, and head are in one line.

Measure 78: <u>Demi-plié</u> on left, bend right knee behind left knee, keeping lower right leg horizontal. Simultaneously close arms to body. Continue to lower body through kneeling on right to sit on right hip, left leg crossed over right knee with left foot flat on floor. Head down, <u>dorsal front bend</u>, hands on floor at sides of body. Turn ninety degrees to left with **back to audience**, knees together and bent, hands on floor behind body, and continue turning ninety degrees to left to sit on left hip, left leg bent ninety degrees in front, right leg bent ninety degrees in back. Finish with **left shoulder to audience**. Hands on floor at sides of body.

Measures 79–80: Keeping left leg bent, turn ninety degrees to left to **face audience**; straighten right leg in air over left. Lie down on floor on left side of body, facing audience. Lie on back and swing right leg in <u>horizontal plane</u> to left, back and to right. Left leg follows right leg, gradually turning whole body to left until lying on floor, with **back to audience**. Close stretched legs together and then turn ninety degrees to right to lie on stomach with **right shoulder to audience**, elbows bent and close to body, hands flat on floor, forehead on floor.

Note: **Measures 81-84 are performed by soloist**. All other dancers lie on floor in position from measure 80.

Measure 81: Swing right leg back and up, turning body to right to sit on left hip with **left shoulder to audience**, both knees bent in right angle, left front, right back, hands to sides touching floor, left hand close to left hip, stretched torso leaning forward, head in one line with back.

Measure 82: Lean farther to front. Through swinging movement stretch right arm front and to left; bend right elbow and make small circle inward with right forearm.

Measure 83: Turning torso ninety degrees to left to **face audience**, support body on left hand, straighten left leg front, prepare right leg so that ball of foot touches floor, lift hips so that weight of body is on left hand with left elbow straight. Straighten right arm directly up. Dorsal backbend and look over left shoulder.

Measure 84: Through stretching right leg up, left foot is on floor with ball of foot to provide support; turn body in air ninety degrees to left so that right side of body is parallel with audience. Lower right leg to left, put legs together, and lower body to floor, finishing lying on stomach with **right shoulder to audience**, elbows bent and close to body, hands flat on floor, forehead on floor.

Note: **In measures 85-88 all other dancers repeat movement of the soloist from measures 81-84.** The soloist lies on floor in position from measure 84.

Note: **Starting with measure 89 all dancers perform together**.

Measure 89: Repeat movement of measure 81 (swing right leg back to sit on hip) to finish with **left shoulder to audience**.

Measure 90: Sitting on left hip, bend legs to right side, and then turn 180 degrees to left on seat to finish with **right shoulder to audience**,. Through impulse raise body to kneel on right knee, left leg bent front in right angle, left flat foot on floor, right arm front horizontal, left arm side horizontal.

Measure 91: Rise to stand on left, right leg back on pique, arms remain in place from previous measure.

Measure 92: Through <u>demi-plié</u> on left and then straightening left knee, slide stretched right leg to close to left leg. Turn 450 degrees (one and a quarter circles) to right on left to **face audience**, finishing in <u>fifth (V) position</u> <u>relevé</u>, right leg front, arms close to body.

Measure 93: Turning forty-five degrees to right to **face right diagonal**, step left front, crossing left over right. Start raising arms to sides.

Measure 94: Turning ninety degrees to left to **face left diagonal**, step right front, crossing right leg over left. Continue raising arms to sides to finish in horizontal.

Measure 95: Cross left leg over right and turn 405 degrees (one and an eighth circles) to right to finish in <u>fifth (V) position</u> <u>relevé</u>, right leg front **facing audience**. Close arms to body and subsequently raise them through front to <u>third position of arms</u>.

Measure 96: Through small <u>develope</u> with left leg, step left front, right <u>leg</u> back <u>on pique</u>. Open arms to sides and close them to body, head down.

Part 3

Starting formation: Dancers are in **one row** with soloist in the middle. Row is as far forward toward audience as possible.

Starting position: **Facing audience**, stand on left, right <u>leg</u> back <u>on pique</u>, arms close to body, head down.

Measure 97: Through <u>demi-plié</u> on left and raising arms side low, continue to close stretched right leg toward left and close arms to body.

Measure 98: Turn 360 degrees to right in <u>relevé</u> to finish **facing audience** in <u>fifth (V) position</u> <u>relevé</u>, right leg front. Arms remain in place from previous measure.

Measure 99: <u>Balance step</u> right, left arm front horizontal, right arm back horizontal, <u>dorsal backbend</u>; look over left shoulder to audience.

Measure 100: Repeat movement of measure 99 to opposite side.

Measure 101: Stepping right side to <u>relevé</u>, <u>soutenu turn</u> 360 degrees to right, arms close to body; finish **facing audience** in <u>fifth (V) position</u> <u>relevé</u>, right leg front.

Measure 102: Through <u>cou-de-pied</u> of right leg and turning forty-five degrees to right, step to side <u>lunge</u> right on right diagonal; right arm describes circle in <u>frontal plane</u> down, left, up, and to right. Head follows movement of right arm. At the end of measure, right arm is side high, palm up; left arm is side low, palm down, and both arms are in one line.

Measure 103: Slide stretched left leg along arc on floor forty-five degrees to front and repeat movement of measure 101 to opposite side.

Measure 104: Repeat movement of measure 102 to opposite side.

Measure 105: Shifting weight to right and turning 135 degrees to right with *left shoulder to audience*, stand on right, slide bent left leg toward right leg, finishing in parallel bend front, ball of left foot next to right foot, right arm to front low, palm down. Through upper arc up and then down front to low, cross left arm over right.

Measure 106: Crossing left leg over right, turn 360 degrees to right to finish in first (I) position with *left shoulder to audience*. Bend elbows to sides and rotate forearms toward body in sagittal plane, opening them front horizontal, palms up, close arms to body.

Measures 107–108: Chaines turns to right in straight line away from audience, arms close to body, fingers touching hips. Finish with *back to audience* in first (I) position. During final chaines, right arm describes arc in horizontal plane low to right, palm up and closes to body.

Measure 109: Turning ninety degrees to left with *left shoulder to audience*, lunge on left, right leg back on flat foot. Stretch left arm to low front. Look over left shoulder. Through impulse from right leg, turn 270 degrees to left, closing right stretched leg toward left leg. Finish with *back to audience* in first (I) position relevé. Close arms to body.

Measure 110: Turn forty-five degrees to left on *back left diagonal*. Crossing right leg over left, step into demi-plié on right; left foot remains stationary, left knee bent, and left leg touching floor with ball of foot. Right arm describes arc from right to left low in front of body, turning palm to right and elbow leading to meet with back of left hand, right palm facing right. Arms cross low, right over left, left palm facing left.

Turned-out develope with left leg to side low, side bend to left. Turn arms 180 degrees so that palms face each other. Continue with left arm to side, right arm in frontal plane to side, up and overhead, finishing with both arms to left parallel with each other, right palm up.

Measures 111–112: Cross left over right. Continue with right arm to finish circle in frontal plane, moving to left and down. Turn 180 degrees to right to *face audience* in first (I) position relevé. Arms side low.

Measure 113: Balance step left, right arm front horizontal, left arm back horizontal, dorsal backbend. Look over right shoulder to audience.

Measure 114: Repeat movement of measure 113 to opposite side.

Measures 115–116: Stepping left side on <u>relevé</u>, <u>soutenu turn</u> 360 degrees to left, arms close to body and then continue through front to <u>third position of arms</u>. Finish **facing audience** in <u>fifth (V) position</u> <u>relevé</u>, left leg front.

Measures 117–120: Repeat movement of measures 113–116 to opposite side with change in measure 120.

> Change: <u>Soutenu turn</u> only 270 degrees to finish with **right shoulder to audience**, standing on left, right parallel bent front on ball of foot next to left foot. Close arms down in <u>sagittal plane</u> from <u>third position of arms</u>, left arm moving front down and right arm moving back down. Head down.

> Note: **Measure 121 is performed by soloist**. All other dancers hold final position of measure 120.

Measure 121: <u>Demi-plié</u> on left, and by stretching left knee with impulse, turn 180 degrees to right to finish with **left shoulder to audience**. Stretching right leg front low, step front right to stand on right, left <u>parallel</u> bent front on ball of foot next to right foot. Arms follow each other in movement; left is about ninety degrees behind right. Movement is up and down in <u>frontal plane</u>. Finish with head down.

Measure 122: Soloist holds final position of measure 121. **All other dancers repeat soloist's movement from measure 121.**

> Note: **Starting with measure 123, all dancers perform together**.

Measure 123:

> Counts 1–2: Repeat leg movements of measure 1, counts 1–2 (through <u>demi-plié</u> on left, step back on right <u>relevé</u>, lift left low). Move arms to sides low and then, turning arms inward, describe arcs from sides to front, wrist leading.

> Count 3: Repeat leg movements of measure 1, count 3 (step left front to <u>demi-plié</u>). Turning arms outward, describe arcs from front to sides, wrist leading.

> Note: Arm movement in measure 123 is done low.

Measure 124: Repeat movement of measure 123 with the following change.

> Change: Lift left leg to horizontal, arm movement in horizontal.

Measure 125: Turning ninety degrees to right with **back to audience**, side <u>lunge</u> right, right arm side, head to right; then right arm arc in <u>frontal plane</u> down, to left, up, and to right. Finish with right arm side, palm up, left arm side. Turn head to right and lean toward right side.

Measure 126: Shifting weight to left, cross right leg over left and turn 270 degrees to left, finishing with **right shoulder to audience**, close arms to body. At the end, arc with right arm in low <u>horizontal plane</u>, from right to left low.

Measure 127: Turn ninety degrees to right to **face audience**, and <u>chaines</u> toward audience. Arms close to body, fingers on hips.

Measure 128: Step left front toward audience, right <u>leg</u> back <u>on pique</u>. At the end, arc with right arm in low <u>horizontal plane</u>, from left to right low. Finish with arms close to body. Head down.

Part 4

Starting formation: Dancers are in one row with soloist in the middle. Row is as far forward toward audience as possible.

Starting position: **Facing audience**, stand on left, right <u>leg</u> back <u>on pique</u>, arms close to body, head down.

Measure 129: Turn 360 degrees to right by first executing slight <u>demi-plié</u> on left and immediately stretching left leg and sliding stretched right leg toward left during turn, to finish **facing audience**, arms close to body.

Measure 130: <u>Balance step</u> right, left arm front horizontal, right arm back horizontal, <u>dorsal backbend</u>. Look over left shoulder to audience.

Measure 131: Repeat movement of measure 130 to opposite side.

Measure 132: Turning ninety degrees to right with **left shoulder to audience**. Step side right on <u>relevé</u>. <u>Soutenu turn</u> 360 degrees to right, finishing with left shoulder to audience in <u>fifth (V) position</u> <u>relevé</u>, right leg front. During entire measure, arms sides low.

Measure 133:

> Count 1: Step right side to <u>demi-plié</u>, turning ninety degrees to right to finish with **back to audience**; stretched left leg describes arc along floor with

toes from back to side to front. Raise left arm back, and moving left arm in horizontal plane, mirror movement of left leg.

Count 2: Step left front on relevé, turning 180 degrees to right to **face audience**, first position of arms.

Count 3: Step right back on relevé. Hold arms in position.

Measure 134:

Count 1: Demi-plié on right, left leg back in cou-de-pied.

Counts 2–3: Small leap back onto left leg; right leg moves through develope back, finishing in lunge on left leg, **facing audience**. Straighten right arm to front horizontal, palm up, left arm to side. At end of measure lean forward with stretched upper body.

Measure 135: Turn forty-five degrees to right to face **right diagonal** and balance step right along **left back diagonal**, arms in frontal plane to right, dorsal side bend to left. Look to right.

Measure 136: Turning forty-five degrees to left to **face audience**, step left on relevé and 360-degree soutenu turn to left, arms through first position to third position.

Measures 137–138: Repeat balance steps from measures 130–131.

Measures 139–140: Repeat movement of measures 133–134 with the following change.

Change: At start, **face audience** and finish with **right shoulder to audience**.

Measure 141: Turn ninety degrees to right to **face audience** and balance step right, arms in frontal plane to right.

Measure 142: Balance step left, arms in frontal plane to left.

Measure 143: Step side right on relevé and 360-degree soutenu turn to right, arms sides low, finish **facing audience**.

Measure 144: Repeat movement of measure 143 with the following change.

Change: Turn only 315 degrees to right, finishing in fifth (V) position, right leg front, **facing left diagonal**.

Measure 145:

> Count 1: Through demi-plié and taking off from both legs, small leap side onto right leg along **right diagonal**, both legs stretched, left leg low side. During leap, left arm low side, look over left shoulder, left arm parallel with left leg, right arm side horizontal.

> Count 2: Turning ninety degrees to right to **face right diagonal**, cross left leg over right, arms close to body.

> Count 3: Shifting weight onto straightened left leg, turn 270 degrees to right on left leg to finish **facing left diagonal**. Right leg continuously brushes floor. During first 180 degrees, right leg is stationary; during last ninety degrees, right leg makes arc along floor with toes to finish standing on left, right leg front on pique.

Measure 146: Continue moving right leg along floor ninety degrees to right. Step right side on relevé along **right diagonal** and make 360-degree soutenu turn to right to finish in fifth (V) position relevé, right leg front, **facing left diagonal**.

Measures 147-148: Repeat movement of measures 145-146 with the following change.

> Change: Soutenu turn 405 degrees (one and an eighth circles) to **face audience** in fifth (V) position relevé, right leg front.

Measure 149: Balance step right, left arm front horizontal, right arm back horizontal, dorsal backbend. Look over left shoulder to audience.

Measure 150: Repeat movement of measure 149 to opposite side.

Measures 151-152: Two soutenu turns to right, parallel with audience. Finish in fifth (V) position relevé, right leg front, **facing audience**, third position of arms.

Measures 153-156: Take four balance steps (right, left, right, left), looking over shoulder (repeat measures 149-150 twice).

Measure 157: Step forward right and soutenu turn 315 degrees to right to finish **facing left diagonal** in fifth (V) position relevé, right leg front. Arms close to body during turn. At end of turn, raise right arm to front horizontal.

Measure 158: Step right front, left back in <u>cou-de-pied</u>; turn ninety degrees to right to **face right diagonal**. Swing right arm in <u>sagittal plane</u> down, back, and then up.

Measures 159: Stretch left <u>leg</u> front <u>to pique</u> and slide to <u>split</u> along **right diagonal**, with side bend to left, left arm stretched left side low toward floor, right arm stretched right side up so that arms are in one line.

Measure 160: Shift weight to left hip to assume the following position: right leg bent on floor at approximately right angle behind body, left leg bent on floor in sharp angle (as much as possible) so that tips of left toes are touching right thigh. Bend forward, forehead on floor, arms close to body, forearms and palms on floor. Pick up scarf.

> Note: Dancers are in one row with soloist in the middle. Row is as far forward toward audience as possible in order to be able to pick up scarf.

Part 5

Starting formation: Dancers are in one line with soloist in the middle. Line is as far forward toward audience as possible.

Starting position: *Facing right diagonal*, sit on left hip, right leg bent on floor at approximately right angle behind body, left leg bent on floor in sharp angle (as much as possible) so that tips of left toes are touching right thigh. Bend forward, forehead on floor, arms close to body, forearms and palms on floor. Scarf held in both hands. (See beginning of dance for how to hold scarf.)

> Note: Music repeats measures 1–32 from the beginning of the dance.

> Note: Legs stationary during measures 1–4.

Measure 1: Straighten body and move stretched arms to front horizontal. Scarf hangs down in <u>frontal plane</u>.

Measure 2: Bend stretched body slightly forward and lower scarf down in <u>frontal plane</u>.

Measures 3–4: Repeat movement of measures 1–2.

Measure 5: Turn forty-five degrees to left to **face audience**. Move right knee to left knee so that dancer is now sitting on left hip, bent knees, legs to right on floor. <u>Arms in frontal plane</u> to right.

Measure 6: Shift weight to knees and kneel on both legs; rise onto knees, knees together, and subsequently turn ninety degrees to left, **right shoulder to audience**, kneeling on right, left leg front, bent at right angle, left foot flat on floor. <u>Figure eight,</u> right arm leading, finishing with arms up; scarf in <u>frontal plane</u> behind body. Rise on left leg, right <u>leg</u> back <u>on pique</u>. Swing arms overhead and front down and diagonally to left, keeping the upper edge of scarf stretched and horizontal. Finish with scarf hanging on left side of body in <u>sagittal plane</u>, hands at hip level, right hand front, left hand back.

Measure 7: Through slight <u>demi-plié</u> and immediately straightening left knee, turn 360 degrees on left leg to right, gradually closing right leg to left, finishing in <u>fifth (V) position relevé</u>, right leg front with **right shoulder to audience**. <u>Figure eight</u>, right arm leading, finishing with arms up, scarf in <u>frontal plane</u> behind body.

Measure 8: Step left front. Swing arms overhead and front down and diagonally to right, keeping the upper edge of scarf stretched and horizontal. Finish with scarf hanging on right side of body in <u>sagittal plane</u>, hands at hip level, left hand front, right hand back.

Measures 9–32: Same as movement of original measures 9–32 **from part 1** of dance with the following changes.

Changes:

Measure 24: Raise arms overhead at end of measure.

Measure 25: Keep arms overhead.

Conclusion

We congratulate you for learning these dances. Hopefully you will find that in a group they're fun. Watching the dancer on YouTube surely must have helped you in understanding how to perform each dance. It must feel good to know that you have accomplished dances which incorporate stretching, reaching, and all kinds of moves to add flexibility and strength to your body. We wish you many hours of fun dancing and staying out of the rocking chair!

Glossary

Airplane arms: Arms straight out to the side in one line, palms facing down; tilt the torso sideways, keeping arms straight.

Arabesque: The position of the body supported on one leg, with the other leg extended behind the body, both knees straight, torso vertical.

Arabesque scale: The position of the body supported on one leg, with the other leg extended behind the body horizontally, both knees straight, torso and head horizontal as an extension of working leg.

Arm sequence: Circle arms in frontal plane close to front of body. Start movement by lowering arms sideways toward torso; cross arms low in front, nearly touching torso; continue movement upward in frontal plane until hands are overhead, palms facing down. Look upward toward palms. Continue movement downward in frontal plane, arms opening to sides, palms up until reaching horizontal; palms turn down and continue movement downward in frontal plane until closing arms to torso on sides.

Arm wave: Arm action in any direction (side, front, or back), with the impulse from the elbow and the forearm following sequentially all the way through the fingertips. Movement should flow. Impulse from the elbow can lead up or down.

Arms in frontal plane to right: Right arm side horizontal, left upper arm nearly vertical, left elbow nearly touching body and bent about ninety degrees, left forearm parallel with right arm in frontal plane.

Arms port de bras: In ballet terms, it is a movement or series of movements made by passing the arm or arms through various positions; carriage of the arms.

Attitude: A position in which the dancer stands (or jumps) on one leg (known as the supporting leg) while the other leg (working leg) is lifted and well turned out, with the knee bent at approximately a ninety-degree angle. The lifted or working leg can be behind (*derrière*), in front (*devant*), or on the side (*à la seconde*) of the body.

Balance step left: Step left to the side, place right foot behind left, shift the weight on the right, and then shift the weight forward again on left.

Balance step forward on right: Rock step, crossing right foot in front of left; lift left foot behind with demi-plié on right and then step back on left and finish with feet together. Use presentational arms on cross step and then move arms to hips on back step.

Canon: Dancers perform the same movement in succession, one dancer after the other (each dancer on an assigned beat in the music).

Cartwheel (on the right): Movement where one moves sideways (in the motion the wheel of a cart would follow) in a straight line, keeping the back straight, placing right hand on the ground followed by left hand as the legs are open sideways as in a V shape and passed over the body while inverted. The left leg then touches the ground first, followed quickly by the right leg. End in a standing position on both legs.

Cat leap right: Taking off from left leg, kick bent right leg (in front attitude) front. While in the air, kick bent left leg (in front attitude) higher than right and land on right leg with left leg still forward.

Chaines: A series of turns (each 180 degrees) as if in a "chain," alternating feet with progression along a straight line or circle. Head is spotting. Usually done in very small steps with straight knees, all steps on toes; it can also be executed on flat feet or in demi-plié.

Chaines with dorsal side bends left: During chaines, keep both arms in one line at all times while alternating dorsal side bends, first to left (while stepping on left), so that right arm is up and left arm is down, and then reverse: side bend to right (while stepping on right), so that left arm is up and right arm is down, and then reverse again. (During chaines, arms appear to describe circles in frontal plane from the viewpoint of audience.)

Charleston step with right: Step right front on demi-plié, heel slightly off the floor with weight on the ball of the foot. Quickly turn right heel out and both knees turn in so that the knees and thighs are touching. Left shin kicks out to horizontal. Step left in front of right leg to repeat to opposite side. This move can be done moving forward or backward.

Chassé step on right: A sliding step in which one foot "chases" and displaces the other. It is a traveling step—literally "to chase." Slide right forward, backward, or sideways followed by sliding left to meet right. First, bend both legs during the slide, and then straighten both legs while left closes to right. It can be done either with springing into the air (when legs meet and straighten) or with relevé (without springing, when legs meet and straighten). It is similar to a gallop (like children pretending to ride a horse).

Circle arms right: Second half of figure eight right, i.e., parts 2 and 3.

Column: A single-file line, perpendicular to audience. One dancer is behind the other, all facing in the same direction.

Cou-de-pied (front or back): A bent and turned-out (or bent and parallel) working leg with toes pointed toward floor is positioned in front of or behind support leg (or on the side) above ankle. If back (or parallel), working leg is touching support leg.

Demi-plié: Standing dancer bends the knee(s) halfway, keeping heel(s) securely on the floor and torso upright.

Develope: A movement in which the working leg is first lifted and then fully extended, passing through attitude (or parallel attitude) position. It can be done in front (*en avant*), to the side (*à la seconde*), or to the back (*derrière*).

Dorsal bend: Movement that occurs in the upper torso. It can be done by arching back, curving forward, or bending sideways.

Explode arms: Both arms shoot out from the center of the body to an upper V shape, with palms facing forward, fingers stretched and apart. This action is performed quickly and with a surprising energy.

Fifth (V) position of legs (right leg front): Starting from first (I) position, keeping legs turned out, move right heel forward to left toe.

Figure eight, right arm leading: (1) Right arm describes arc from right to front while left arm moves front to low right, dorsal front bend. (2) Right arm continues left up while left arm is still on right side in front of body, dorsal side bend to left. (3) Right arm continues back in horizontal plane behind body, finishing right up; left arm moves to left up. Straighten torso. Movement is continuous during this configuration, and left arm follows movement of right arm slightly later.

First position of arms: Position arms in front of the waistline parallel to the navel; arms are slightly curved and fingertips are pointing toward one another.

First (I) position of legs: Standing, heels together, toes pointed out, feet in a V formation.

Fouette with right leg: Swing straight right leg front to horizontal; left supporting leg is also straight. Turn quickly 180 degrees to left on supporting left leg, keeping right leg stationary in the air. Finish with right leg in arabesque.

Fourth (IV) position of legs (right leg front): Starting from fifth (V) position, keeping legs turned out, move right turned-out foot forward to a distance of approximately one foot, with equal weight on each foot.

Frontal plane: Refers to the space or action occurring in the vertical plane in the front of or behind the body.

Gallop: Chassé with springing into the air.

Grapevine step to right: Side step right, step left across in front of right (in front of support leg), side step right, step left across behind right (behind the support leg); repeat the sequence.

Heel drag backward right: Step back right on diagonal to demi-plié, shifting right hip out and dragging left heel on floor toward body (right hip leading the movement), left knee straight, left foot flexed. Hands in fists are placed on hips. Straight torso tilts forward with each step, head in line with torso.

Hop with wiggles: Spring into the air on both legs while stretching the legs toward the floor. Land on both legs with knees bent and feet slightly apart. Move the shoulders, alternating front and back while the arms hang down loose. Allow the arms to react freely and naturally to the shoulders moving, causing them to "wiggle" in the air.

Horizontal plane: Refers to the space or action occurring in plane parallel with the floor. It can be at any level, including above the head.

Jeté: Small leap with straight legs, taking off from one leg and landing on the other.

Jump from both to both: From demi-plié, spring from both legs. In the air one leg bends at knee, and then straighten both legs again and put them together, finally landing on both.

Lunge (front, side, back): Support leg is in demi-plié while the other leg is straightened on pique back, side, or front. The weight of the body is on the support leg.

Leg on pique: Stretched working leg to touch floor with toes (front, side, back).

Parallel: Working leg not turned out, if this term is connected with another dance term (e.g., attitude, passé, etc.).

Parallel attitude: Attitude when working leg is not turned out.

Parallel demi-plié: Demi-plié on both legs (or one), feet (foot) pointed straight ahead. If on both legs, it can be done with legs together or apart.

Parallel passé: Passé forward when working leg is pointed straight ahead (not turned out).

Partial split right: Split as defined under split right, but weight is shifted to right hip. One or both legs can be bent.

Pas de basque to right: Start in demi-plié on left, with right leg bent in front, right toes touching floor; circle right toes on the floor to right and do small leap onto right foot, turning head slightly to right. Cross left in front of right on relevé; shift weight onto left and then back to right into demi-plié.

Passé: Standing on supporting leg, the working leg is bent so that the thigh is horizontal and foot is placed at knee level of supporting leg.

Pivot on right to right: Step forward right into demi-plié, shifting weight on it and leaving left foot in place on floor. By quickly straightening right knee with relevé on right and spotting, rotate to right on the ball of right foot to the desired degree of rotation.

Pivot step on right: Maintaining left leg in the same place the whole time, step with right forward and turn 180 degrees to left; weight is on the right leg. Switch weight of the body to the left leg, step right forward passing beyond the left leg, put weight on the right, and turn to the left 180 degrees. Repeat.

Plié: Standing dancer bends the knee(s) completely, keeping torso upright.

Port de bras: Carriage of the arms. A movement or series of movements made by passing the arm or arms through various positions.

Prancing: Hop onto right and put weight on right foot; simultaneously lift left knee in parallel front attitude and then repeat to left. Legs are sharp and toes point as soon as they leave the floor. While prancing, torso remains straight, elbows are bent in sharp angle, elbows and upper arms touching body, forearms front, wrists bent down, and hands are hanging.

Presentational arms: Starting from first position arms, gesture the arms open to the sides in the horizontal plane with palms facing up.

Rainbow step to right: Side step together right with windmill arms to right.

Rainbow turn: Windmill arms while executing a pivot step.

Relevé: Commonly used in ballet, relevé is a movement in which the dancer rises on the tips of the toes or on the balls of the feet. This movement can be performed on both legs simultaneously or on one leg (with the other foot not touching the floor).

Row: Single line of dancers, parallel with audience. One dancer next to the other, all facing in the same direction.

Sagittal plane: Refers to the space or action occurring in the vertical plane on the sides of the body.

Scissor leap right: Taking off from left leg, kick right leg straight front up. While in the air, kick left leg higher than right leg and land on right leg with left leg still forward.

Second position of arms: Arms extended horizontally out to the sides.

Second (II) position (of legs): Legs turned out and in a wider stance (wider than shoulder width apart), equal weight on each foot.

Shoulder stand: Lie down on back. Bend knees up over chest, legs together. Gradually straighten legs and push hips forward until reaching vertical alignment, resting weight on shoulders. Support lower back with palms or straighten arms along floor with palms down.

Side body wave right: Standing on left, right leg to side on pique. Bend left knee to demi-plié; shift the left hip to side so that torso bends to right. Gradually shift weight of body onto right leg, so that both legs are in second (II) position demi-plié. Push right hip to side so that torso bends to left and shift weight onto right leg in demi-plié. Straighten right knee, finishing standing on right with left leg side on pique. During the whole sequence, keep torso vertical (no movement forward or backward). This movement is performed smoothly and sequentially.

Soutenu turn to right: Prepare right leg side on pique, left leg in demi-plié. Step right side on relevé and close stretched left leg to right to fifth (V) position relevé, left leg front, turning 360 degrees to right in relevé to finish in fifth (V) position relevé, right leg front.

Split right: Sitting on the floor, extend right leg front and left leg back. Keep hips from rotating and torso vertical.

Spotting: A term given to the movement of the head and focusing of the eyes while turning. The dancer chooses a spot in front at eye level, and as the turn is made toward the spot, the head is the last to leave and the first to arrive at the spot as the body completes the turn. This rapid movement or snap of the head gives the impression that the face is always turned forward and prevents the dancer from becoming dizzy.

Stag leap: Jeté as defined above but with the front leg bent.

Step together with right: Step right to side, forward, or back and close left leg to right.

Support leg or standing leg: The leg on which full body weight is being supported.

Third position of arms: Arms raised up, elbows slightly bent, palms facing down, fingers of one hand nearly touching fingers of the other. Arms are not directly overhead but slightly to front, so that if dancer looks up, she looks directly into palms.

Windmill arms right: Starting with both arms down on left side of body, torso turned to left, right arm leads in frontal plane, reaching high and to the right side; left follows in same plane. Finish with both arms down on right side of body, torso turned to right. Head follows arm movements.

Working leg: The leg doing the action and not serving as support.

Links to Dances

Dance	YouTube Web Pages
Dance 1 "Who Cares?"	http://www.youtube.com/watch?v=g3SPyVK2mXA&feature=share&list=PLMXzOm_ewb6nKoy7JABHy9PsWC6fJ3xck
Dance 2 "Trekking"	http://www.youtube.com/watch?v=n8OXuoAgsik&feature=share&list=PLMXzOm_ewb6nKoy7JABHy9PsWC6fJ3xck&index=2
Dance 3 "Reflections"	http://www.youtube.com/watch?v=SAjzVVKI7Jg&feature=share&list=PLMXzOm_ewb6nKoy7JABHy9PsWC6fJ3xck&index=4
Dance 4 "Innocence Waltz"	http://www.youtube.com/watch?v=z2Up1aqwVxw&list=PLMXzOm_ewb6nKoy7JABHy9PsWC6fJ3xck&feature=share&index=5
Dance 5 "Portraits"	http://www.youtube.com/watch?v=i-Fn79f_iUw&list=PLMXzOm_ewb6nKoy7JABHy9PsWC6fJ3xck&feature=share&index=6
Dance 6 "Clown Dance"	http://www.youtube.com/watch?v=BVQu227ZzMM&list=PLMXzOm_ewb6nKoy7JABHy9PsWC6fJ3xck&feature=share&index=7
Dance 7 "Remembrance"	http://www.youtube.com/watch?v=NLg3oSQoOVE&feature=share&list=PLMXzOm_ewb6nKoy7JABHy9PsWC6fJ3xck&index=8
Dance 8 "Muffin Rag"	http://www.youtube.com/watch?v=WcFnEDClR-Q&list=PLMXzOm_ewb6nKoy7JABHy9PsWC6fJ3xck&feature=share&index=9
Dance 9 "Snowfall"	http://www.youtube.com/watch?v=NFSFJdoJphg&feature=share&list=PLMXzOm_ewb6nKoy7JABHy9PsWC6fJ3xck&index=10
Dance 10 "Medieval Waltz" Part 1	http://www.youtube.com/watch?v=W5UGEn-bneU&list=PLMXzOm_ewb6nKoy7JABHy9PsWC6fJ3xck&feature=share&index=11
Dance 10 "Medieval Waltz" Part 2	http://www.youtube.com/watch?v=yisx3fl6Pwo&feature=share&list=PLMXzOm_ewb6nKoy7JABHy9PsWC6fJ3xck&index=12
Dance 10 "Medieval Waltz" Part 3	http://www.youtube.com/watch?v=stWAFItLcNE&feature=share&list=PLMXzOm_ewb6nKoy7JABHy9PsWC6fJ3xck&index=13
Dance 10 "Medieval Waltz" Part 4	http://www.youtube.com/watch?v=aHtyMXzUUts&list=PLMXzOm_ewb6nKoy7JABHy9PsWC6fJ3xck&feature=share&index=14
Dance 10 "Medieval Waltz" Part 5	http://www.youtube.com/watch?v=Bsovog1Ye60&list=PLMXzOm_ewb6nKoy7JABHy9PsWC6fJ3xck&feature=share&index=15